ART
OF
ANTIQUE
BEADING

This book introduces chic accessories and bags with an antique style theme. Uplifting the standard of handmade fashion goods, their individual qualities shine.

CONTENTS

Beautiful Accessories to Decorate Collars and Neclines *p.2*
Necklace ● Lariat
Choker ● Pendant

Rings Which Produce Elegant Gestures *p.12*
Ring

Enchanting Accessories which Elicit Whispers *p.18*
Clip on earrings and pierced earrings

Accessories to Add Color *p.22*
Pin

Accessories Which Casually Assert Femininity on the Wrist *p.24*
Bracelet

Stylish Accessories for Making Hairstyles Gorgeous *p.26*
Barret ● Comb ● Hairband

Go With Accessory Style Bead Bags *p.30*
Bag ● Pouch
Mini Bag ● Amulet Bag

Beads to Yearn For Total Coordination *p.36*
Accessory Set

Technique Guide *p.87*

Beautiful Accessories
to Decorate Collars and Necklines

Drape naturally at the neckline, tie,
use long version to wrap once around the neck,
fold in half to drape the short end,
or match to a fashionable collar.
Arranging the lariat is fun.
Using slightly heavy "metal beads"
makes for comfort of wearing
as for an effective design.

Lariat

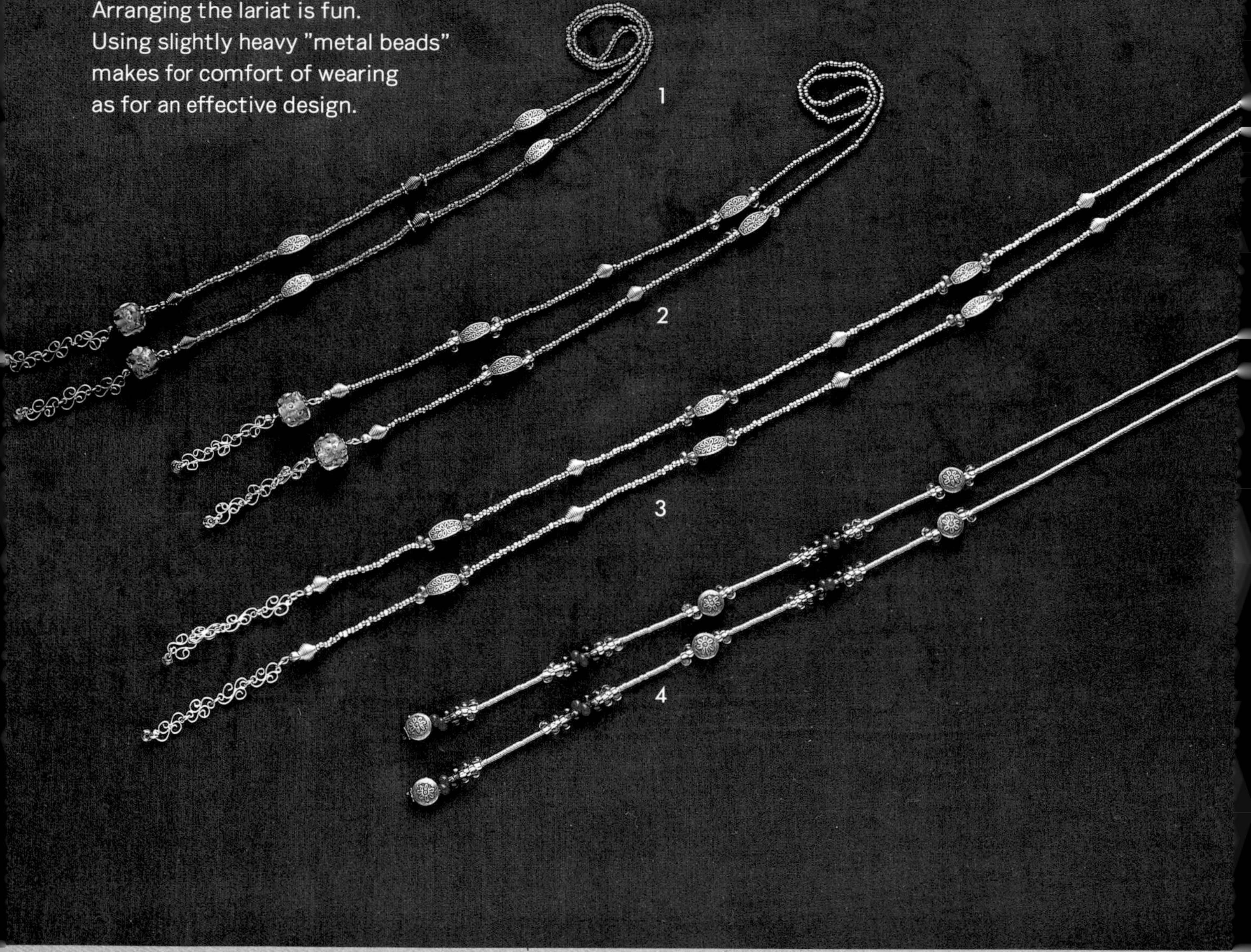

1

2

3

4

Directions page 3

1 Lariat

Materials

Toho Beads / Mill Hill Beads

3 cut beads – metallic (CR244) 441 beads

Decora beads – blue (a-5616) 2 beads

Maga tama beads – blue (M23/4mm) 2 beads

Metal beads – antique silver (a-7201SF) 4 beads

Metal parts, joint – bronze (A) 6 pieces, bronze (B) 4 pieces, antique silver 4 pieces

Bead cap – antique silver 4 pieces

Beading thread – black 180cm/70 ¾ inches

Jump ring – bronze (3.8mm round) 8 pieces

Eye pin – antique silver (30mm) 2 pieces

Bead tip – bronze 2 pieces

Craft glue

Directions – String beads on doubled thread 90cm/35 ½ inches long. Finish the end with a bead tip. Thread beads on the eye pin. Use jump rings to connect the parts.

Size – 70.5cm /27 ¾ inches

2 Materials

Toho Beads / Mill Hill Beads

3 cut beads – bronze (CR221) 441 beads

Decora beads – green (a-5618) 2 beads

Maga tama beads – amber (M22/4mm) 18 beads

Metal beads – antique gold (a-7201GF) 4 beads

Metal parts, joint – gold (A) 6 pieces, gold (B) 4 pieces

Bead cap – antique silver 4 pieces

Beading thread – black 180cm/70 ¾ inches

Jump ring – gold (3.8mm round) 8 pieces

Eye pin – antique gold (30mm) 2 pieces

Bead tip – gold 2 pieces

Craft glue

Directions Same as for lariat #1.

Size – 73cm/28 ¾ inches

3 Materials

Toho Beads / Mill Hill Beads

Royal beads 3 cut – silver (CR713) 450 beads

Maga tama beads – blue purple and transparent (M348/4mm) 26 beads

Metal beads – antique silver (a-7201SF) 6 beads

Metal parts, joint – silver (A), silver (B) 8 pieces each

Beading thread – white 220cm/86 ½ inches

Jump ring – silver (3.8mm round) 10 pieces

Bead tip – silver 2 pieces

Craft glue

Directions Make using the techniques for lariat #1.

Size – 92cm/36 ½ inches

4 Materials

Toho Beads / Mill Hill Beads

3 cut beads – black (CR491) 2 beads

TB beads – bronze (TB262) 360 beads

Maga tama beads – 4mm transparent (M21) 36 beads, amber (M22) brown (MO202) 20 beads each, bright red (M46) 12 beads

Metal beads – antique gold (a-7203GF) 6 beads

Bead cap – antique silver 2 pieces

Beading thread – black 180cm/70 ¾ inches

Craft glue

Directions – Thread beads on 2 strands of 90cm/35 ½ inches length thread. Thread the end back through the beads. Tie firmly at the position shown on diagram. Secure with craft glue.

Size – 71cm/28 inches

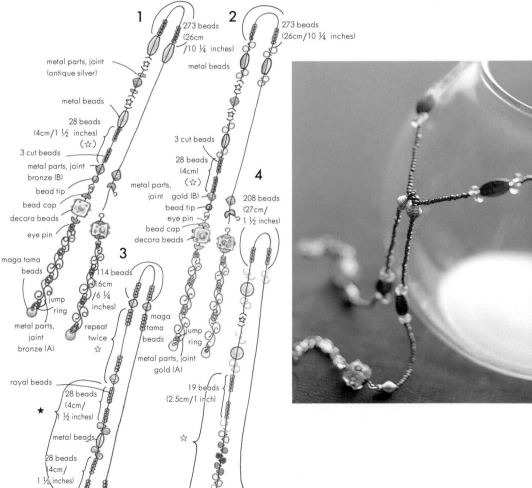

1

273 beads (26cm /10 ¼ inches)

metal parts, joint (antique silver)

metal beads

28 beads (4cm/1 ½ inches) (☆)

3 cut beads

metal parts, joint bronze (B)

bead tip

bead cap

decora beads

eye pin

maga tama beads

jump ring

metal parts, joint bronze (A)

royal beads

28 beads (4cm/ 1 ½ inches)

★

metal beads

28 beads (4cm/ 1 ½ inches)

metal parts, joint silver (B)

bead tip

metal parts, joint silver (A)

jump ring

maga tama beads

2

273 beads (26cm/10 ¼ inches)

metal beads

3 cut beads

28 beads (4cm) (☆)

metal parts, joint gold (B)

bead tip

eye pin

bead cap

decora beads

3

114 beads (16cm /6 ¼ inches)

repeat twice ☆

maga tama beads

metal parts, joint gold (A)

jump ring

19 beads (2.5cm/1 inch)

☆

19 beads (2.5cm/1 inch)

TB beads

transparent

amber

brown

bright red

metal beads

bead cap

3 cut beads

4

208 beads (27cm/ 1 ½ inches)

maga tama beads

Thread end through the beads once again. Tie at the heart twice and secure with craft glue.

Lariat

#6 is worn choker like around the neck, kept in place at the intersection by the bead ball, leaving the other string to dangle.

Lariat

A lariat to fit retro styles such as Garconne and Mog. Makes for a gorgeous neckline.

5   6

7   8   9

Directions page 42

Directions page 43

Choker

three dimensional type choker snuggles the neck. As it is tied
e back with a ribbon, it suits short hair or upswept hairstyles.

Choker

This type lays flat on the neckline.
Tie the ribbon as you like.

10

11

12

13

14

Directions page 44

Directions pages 44～45

Necklace

The addition of contrasting style, large beads makes this many stranded necklace more gorgeous.
It's like adding a blossom to a chic outfit.

15

16

Directions page 46

Necklace and Bracelet

A number of simple strings of beads are put together for a gorgeously designed necklace and bracelet. The bracelet is merely a shorter version. The gradation from purple to pink is graceful and lustrous.

Directions page 47

19

20

21

22

Directions pages 47~49

8

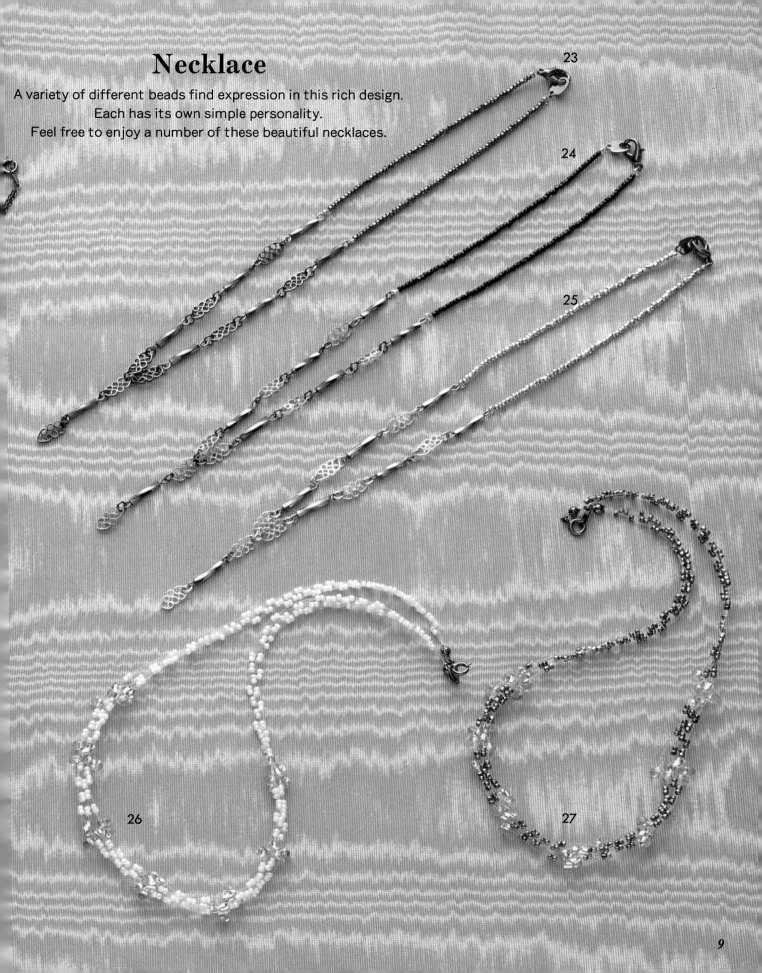

Necklace

A variety of different beads find expression in this rich design.
Each has its own simple personality.
Feel free to enjoy a number of these beautiful necklaces.

23

24

25

26

27

Pendant

Pendant #29 treats a purchased perfume bottle with flowers. Functional and elegant.

28

29

Directions pages 49～50

The flower image wreath of #28 is the same as broach #74 and #75 on pages 22～23.

Directions page 51

Pendant

A pendant cross treated with flowers.
This chic design has a dignified air.

30

31

Choker

Cute floral chokers using antique colors.
One light the other dark.

32

33

Directions page 52

Ring

Using different colors creates different looks.
The hard, round spheres bloom magnificently like a large flower.

34

35

36

34 Ring

Materials

Toho Beads / Mill Hill Beads

Small round beads – pink (205) 56 beads, bronze (222) 42 beads, metallic pink (556) 12 beads

Semi-precious beads – purple (a-1544/spherical 4mm) 6 beads

Crystal cut beads – amethyst (J-54/4mm/#8) 6 beads

Acrylic beads – purple (a-230/spherical 6mm) 1 bead

Nylon thread – (0.2mm diameter) 60cm – 23 ½ inches

Craft glue

Directions – String beads on nylon thread. Make rows 1 & 2, turn over to make round 3. Before closing round 3, insert a bead inside. Continue making ring. Tie nylon thread off tightly and secure with craft glue.

Size – Interior diameter 5.5cm/2 ¼ inches

35 Materials

Toho Beads / Mill Hill Beads

Small round beads – black (49) 110 beads

Black pearl – 4mm – 6 beads, 6mm – 1 bead

Crystal cut beads – black (J-54/4mm/#10) 6 beads

Nylon thread – (0.2mm diameter) 60cm/ 23 ¼ inches

Craft glue

Directions – Same as for ring #34.

Size – Inside diameter 5.5cm/2 ¼ inches

36 Materials

Toho Beads / Mill Hill Beads

Small round beads – bronze (221) 42 beads, brown (941) 38 beads, amber (2) 18 beads, gold (557) 12 beads

Semi-precious beads – brown (a-1546/sphere 4mm) 6 beads

Crystal cut beads – topaz (J-54/4mm/#3) 6 beads

Frosted gold pearl – (6mm) 1 bead

Nylon thread – (0.2mm diameter) 60cm/ 23 ½ inches

Craft glue

Directions – Same as for ring #34.

Size – Inside diameter 5.5cm/2 ¼ inches

First Round

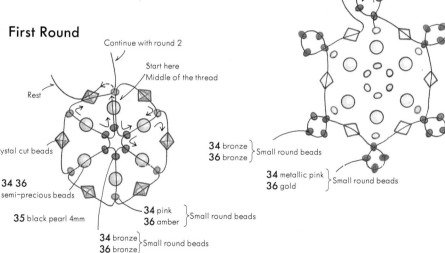

Continue with round 2

Start here
Middle of the thread

Rest

Crystal cut beads

34 36
semi-precious beads

35 black pearl 4mm

34 bronze / **36** bronze — Small round beads

34 pink / **36** amber — Small round beads

34 bronze / **36** bronze — Small round beads

2nd Round

34 bronze / **36** bronze — Small round beads

34 metallic pink / **36** gold — Small round beads

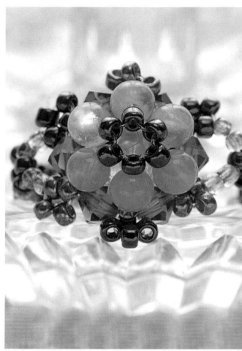

3rd round

(Turn over, thread through the beads of round #1)

Beads from round 2

Continuing on from the 2nd round

Nylon thread resting from round 1

Before closing completely, insert bead

34 acrylic beads
35 black pearl beads 6mm
36 frosted gold pearl

Tie off firmly and secure with craft glue

Beads from round 1

Continue making ring

34 pink / **36** amber — Small round beads

34 pink / **36** brown — Small round beads

34 bronze / **36** bronze — Small round beads

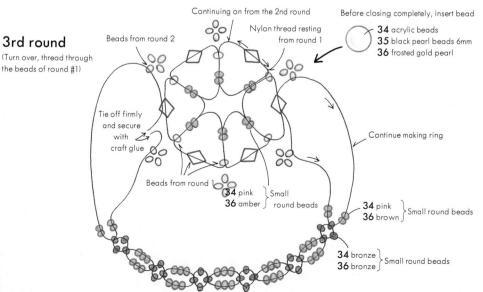

Ring

A dome shaped ring made of half moon pearl beads surrounded by small beads. A voluminous design.

The diamond shaped design at the base of the finger is fresh. A ring which has a metallic feeling.

A flower bead woven ring.
All have a retro color scheme that will glitter on your finger. A design worth the effort.

A simply, designed ring using bugle beads.
A ring to neatly show off the finger.

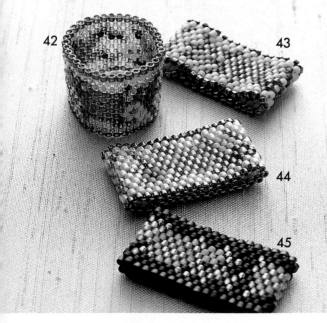

Directions page 53～56
#45 page 65

Ring

A cute, woven bead ring
that looks like a small crown.

Directions page 56

Ring

A ring knit with wire
featuring a single bead.

Ring

Large flocked beads
wrapped in wire form a singular ring.

Directions page 57

Directions page 57

Ring

A voluminous ring made with a mix of crystal-colored maga tama beads.

Ring

A cute and simple design fit for casual style.

56

58

57

59

Directions page 57

Directions page 65

Clip Earrings
and
Pierced Earrings

60

Earrings that sway.
Clip earrings suitable for calm colors
and casual silver pierced earrings.
With one method different effects
can be enjoyed.

61

62

Directions page 19

60 Pierced Earrings

Materials

Toho Beads / Mill Hill Beads

Maga tama beads – brown (M0202/4mm) 8 beads

Pierced earring findings – silver (hook) 1 pair

Beading wire – silver (0.75mm diameter) 30cm/11 ¾ inches

Jump ring - silver (3.8mm round) 12 pieces

Directions – Bend wire as in diagram. Attach beads and earring findings with jump rings.

Size – Refer to diagram.

61 Earrings

Materials

Toho Beads / Mill Hill Beads

Maga tama beads – light pink (M171/4mm) 8 beads

Earring findings with hinges and screws – antique gold (a-542GF) 1 pair

Beading wire – moss green (0.75mm diameter) 30cm/11 ¾ inches

Jump ring – antique gold (3.8mm round) 12 pieces

Directions – Make the same as for #60 pierced earrings.

Size – Refer to diagram

62

Materials

Toho Beads / Mill Hill Beads

Maga tama beads – flourescent blue green (M307/4mm) 8 beads

Earring finding with hinges and screws – antique bronze (a-542DF) 1 pair

Beading wire – bronze (0.75mm diameter) 30cm/11 ¾ inches

Jump ring – antique bronze (3.8mm round) 12 pieces

Directions – Make the same as for #60 pierced earrings.

Size – Refer to diagram.

60

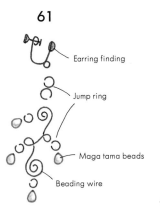

Pierced earring finding

Jump ring

Maga tama beads

Beading wire

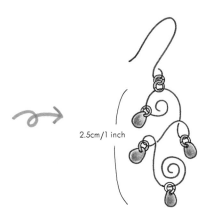

2.5cm/1 inch

61

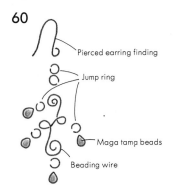

Earring finding

Jump ring

Maga tama beads

Beading wire

62

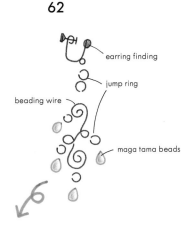

earring finding

jump ring

beading wire

maga tama beads

Changing **#60** pierced earrings to clip ons. Make the same way.

earring finding

How to bend wire (Actual size)
60 pierced earrings
61·62 clip earrings

Make 2 pieces

Earring

63

64

#64, #65, #66, #69 and #79 are earrings which show off your favorite beads in simple settings. #63 and #67 are the earring version of ring on page 14. #68 uses the often seen bead ball as its focus.

65

66

67

68

69

70

Directions pages 58〜59

Earring

So simple to make and yet so fashionable.
Make using your favorite beads freely. A good project for the beginner.

71

72

73

Directions page 60

Accessories to Add Color

74

#74 & #75 are wreath images made by assembling the flower parts.
This charming, cascading type reveals different facets as it sways.
#76 & #77 surround a store bought cameo with beads.
For that "I made it myself" fresh sense.
#80 & #81 are retro flower pins.
On page 34, the flower is paired with a bag.

76

77

Directions pages 60~64

80

81

Pin

75

#78 & #79 are bouquets type pins with ribbons attached.
For dressing up gorgeously.
#82 & #83 are small corsages type pins.
A design with a lovely feeling.

78

79

82

83

Accessories which casually assert femininity on the wrist.

Bracelet

A bracelet made with nylon thread
that fits the arm.
The style popularly called "tattoo band"
was scattered with beads to produce
an understated look.

85

84

Directions page 65

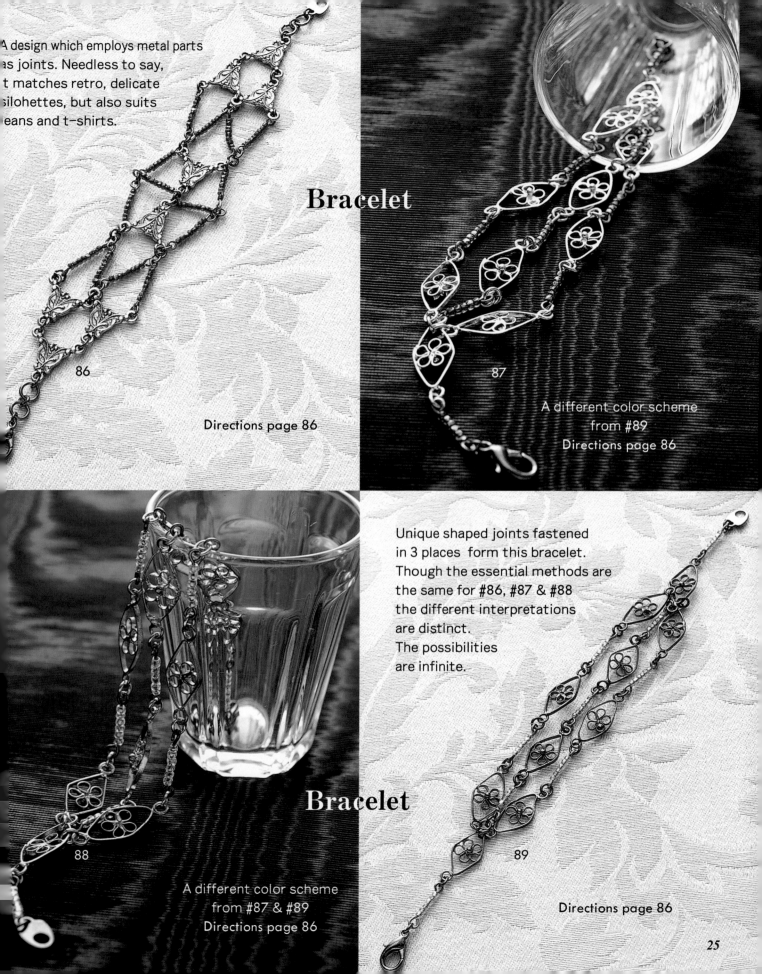

A design which employs metal parts as joints. Needless to say, it matches retro, delicate silohettes, but also suits jeans and t-shirts.

Bracelet

86

Directions page 86

87

A different color scheme from #89
Directions page 86

88

A different color scheme from #87 & #89
Directions page 86

Unique shaped joints fastened in 3 places form this bracelet. Though the essential methods are the same for #86, #87 & #88 the different interpretations are distinct. The possibilities are infinite.

Bracelet

89

Directions page 86

Stylish Accessories for Making Hairstyles Gorgeous

Barrette

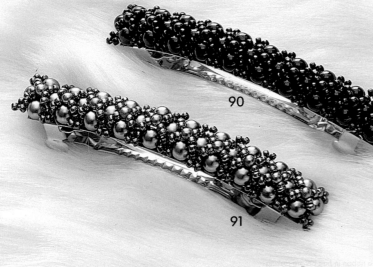

2 kinds of beads, #90 uses one color
#91 uses two colors, for an orthodox barrette
which matches any fashion style.
#92 is made with ribbon, bead rose and flowers
for a feminine hair accessory.

Comb

Graceful and simple as it is,
this comb yields a rich look
and an impression making hairstyle.
Recommended for upswept hairstyles
using multiple hair ornaments.

Directions #90～92 page 72, #93 & #94 page 86

Barrettes

90

Materials

Toho Beads / Mill Hill Beads

Small round beads – black (49) 168 beads

Black pearl (5mm) – 31 beads, 3mm – 10 beads

Nylon thread – (0.3mm diameter) 170cm/ 67 inches

Barrette back – gold (85mm) 1

Directions – Loop thread through barrette and thread beads as in diagram.

Size – Refer to diagram.

91

Materials

Toho Beads / Mill Hill Beads

Small round beads – bronze (222) 88 beads

Royal beads, small round – pink (605) 80 beads

Dark gun metal pearl (5mm) – 31 beads

Colored pearl – bronze (3mm) 10 beads

Nylon thread – (0.3mm diameter) 170cm/ 67 inches

Barrette back – silver (85mm) 1

Craft glue

Directions – Make as for #90 barrette.

Size – Refer to diagram.

92

Materials

Toho Beads / Mill Hill Beads

TB beads – pink (TB-177) 112 beads

Small round beads – amber (2) 88 beads

Maga tama beads – silver lined transparent (M21/4mm) 3 beads

Gold enamel pearl – 8mm, 7mm, 3mm 1 each

Colored pearl – bronze (4mm) 1 bead

Semi-precious beads – tiger's eye (a-1546) 1 bead

Colored wire – (0.35~0.37mm diameter) gold 80cm/31 ½ inches

Nylon thread – (0.3mm diameter) 100cm/ 39 ½ inches

Bead cap (large) – antique gold 2 pieces

Bead cap (small) – antique gold 1 piece

Head pin – antique gold (22mm) 2 pins

Jump rings – bronze (3.8mm round) 2 pieces

Pierced surface barrette – silver (85mm) 1

Wired ribbon – varigated brown (25mm width) 45cm, pale orange and green (25mm width) 25cm/9 ¾ inches, olive green (25mm width) 20cm/7 ¾ inches, brown (15mm width) 10cm/4 inches, metallic and orange (15mm width) 5cm/2 inches

Polyester stuffing

Directions – Secure nylon thread on barrette finding and then string beads as shown in diagram.

Size – Refer to diagram.

90·91 Barrette

Row 1

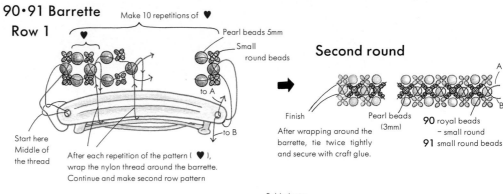

Make 10 repetitions of ♥

Pearl beads 5mm

Small round beads

to A

to B

Start here Middle of the thread

After each repetition of the pattern (♥), wrap the nylon thread around the barrette. Continue and make second row pattern

Second round

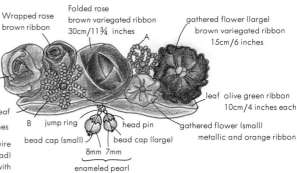

Finish

After wrapping around the barrette, tie twice tightly and secure with craft glue.

Pearl beads (3mm)

90 royal beads – small round

91 small round beads

92 Barrette

Make the individual flowers, leaves and hanging beads. Secure the hanging beads to the bottom middle of the pierced barrette with a jump ring. Then, leaves, followed by ribbon flowers and beaded flowers, in that order.

Wrapped rose brown ribbon

Folded rose brown variegated ribbon 30cm/11 ¾ inches

gathered flower (large) brown variegated ribbon 15cm/6 inches

Wrapped rose pale orange and green ribbon

leaf

A

leaf olive green ribbon 10cm/4 inches each

gathered flower (small) metallic and orange ribbon

B   jump ring   head pin

bead cap (small)   bead cap (large)

8mm 7mm

enameled pearl

[Flowers A·B] Colored wire 40cm/15 ¾ inches

Bring wire up at ★. Thread bead on wire (A colored pearl, B semi-precious bead) String back through ☆ and twist with other wire.

Insert in pierced surface and twist A & B wires to secure on back.

One petal is made with 14 TB beads for A and 11 small round beads for B

[Making a leaf] (Make 2)

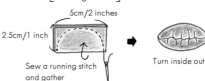

5cm/2 inches

2.5cm/1 inch

Sew a running stitch and gather

Turn inside out.

[Making a Folded Rose]

Fold a ribbon in half before making

1.   2.   3.   4.   5.   6.   7.

8.   9.   10.   11.

Thread

8. Repeat 6 & 7 matching the corners each time. Fold until the end.

9. Turn over. Take the first triangle folded, fold out and stuff in the center hole.

10. Turn right side up. Hold in both hands as shown in diagram. Use both index fingers to push from the back, in the middle while making the bud seem to blossom.

11. Put shape in order. Add some stuffing to hole. Sew across the edges to keep the shape from disintegrating.

[Making a small gathered flower]

1cm / ½ inch

5cm /2 inches

Sew a running stitch and gather.

Sew a 3mm enameled gold pearl together with flower to pierced surface finding.

[Making a large gathered flower]

1.3 cm

15cm/ 6 inches

Sew a running stitch and gather

[Making a rolled rose]

① Fold on an angle before starting to roll.

② Continue rolling while folding outwards

③ Roll to the end and sew to secure.

Sew 3 maga tama beads to the rose and secure on pierced surface finding.

Combs #93 & #94 on page 86.

Barrette

Though simple, small designs,
these 3 barrettes are big on personality.

95

96

97

Directions page 66

Hair Band
and
Barrette

The hairband is a handy accessory for formal,
dress up occasions.
The oversized barrette proclaims its existence.
The brightness of the beads yields
an understated, sparkling elegance.

98

99

Directions pages 66 & 67

Go With Accessory Style Bead Bags

Bag

100

101

Bugle beads scattered like fringe.
Art noveau style curved trimming
decorates a chic bag.
Just holding it gives one a refined feeling.

Directions page 31

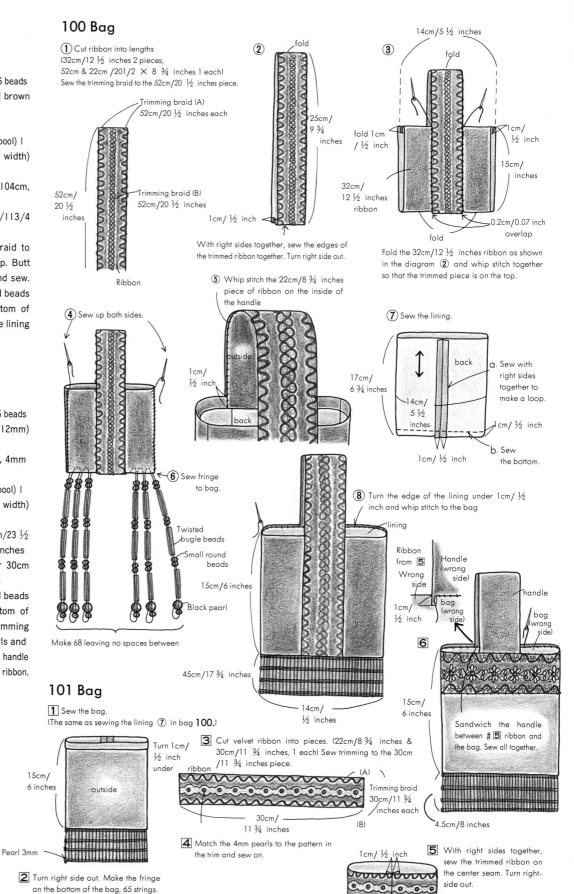

00 Bag

Materials

Toho Beads / Mill Hill Beads

Small round beads – black (49) 476 beads

Twisted bugle beads – frosted brown (702/12mm) 204 beads

Black pearl – (3mm) 68 beads

Beading thread – black (100m spool) 1

Velvet ribbon – black (48mm width) 138cm/54 1/4 inches

Trimming braid – green (A)104cm, green (B) 52cm/20 1/2 inches

Lining fabric – 30cm × 17cm/113/4 × 6 3/4 inches

Directions – Sew trimming braid to the ribbon and sew into a loop. Butt side ribbons against the loop and sew. Sew the sides together. Thread beads on string and sew to the bottom of the bag to make fringe. Sew the lining and whip stitch together.

Size – Refer to diagram.

01

Materials

Toho Beads / Mill Hill Beads

Small round beads – black (49) 455 beads

Twisted bugle beads – grey (81/12mm) 195 beads

Black pearl – 3mm – 65 beads, 4mm – 12 beads

Beading thread – black (100m spool) 1

Velvet ribbon – black (48mm width) 52cm/20 1/2 inches

Trimming braid – black (A) 60cm/23 1/2 inches, (B) black 30cm/11 3/4 inches

Fabric for bag – black velour 30cm ×17cm /113/4 × 6 3/4 inches

Directions – Make bag. Thread beads on string and sew to the bottom of the bag to make fringe. Sew trimming braid to the ribbon, attach pearls and sew into a loop. Insert the ribbon handle between the bag and the trimmed ribbon. Sew together.

Size – Refer to diagram.

100 Bag

① Cut ribbon into lengths (32cm/12 1/2 inches 2 pieces, 52cm & 22cm /201/2 × 8 3/4 inches 1 each) Sew the trimming braid to the 52cm/20 1/2 inches piece.

Trimming braid (A) 52cm/20 1/2 inches each

Trimming braid (B) 52cm/20 1/2 inches

52cm/ 20 1/2 inches

Ribbon

② fold

25cm/ 9 3/4 inches

1cm/ 1/2 inch

With right sides together, sew the edges of the trimmed ribbon together. Turn right side out.

⑤ Whip stitch the 22cm/8 3/4 inches piece of ribbon on the inside of the handle

outside

1cm/ 1/2 inch

back

④ Sew up both sides.

⑥ Sew fringe to bag.

Twisted bugle beads

Small round beads

Black pearl

Make 68 leaving no spaces between

③ 14cm/5 1/2 inches

fold

fold 1cm / 1/2 inch

32cm/ 12 1/2 inches ribbon

1cm/ 1/2 inch

15cm/ inches

fold

0.2cm/0.07 inch overlap

Fold the 32cm/12 1/2 inches ribbon as shown in the diagram ② and whip stitch together so that the trimmed piece is on the top.

⑦ Sew the lining.

17cm/ 6 3/4 inches

14cm/ 5 1/2 inches

1cm/ 1/2 inch

back

a. Sew with right sides together to make a loop.

1cm/ 1/2 inch

b. Sew the bottom.

⑧ Turn the edge of the lining under 1cm/ 1/2 inch and whip stitch to the bag

lining

Ribbon from ⑤ Wrong side

1cm/ 1/2 inch

Handle (wrong side)

bag (wrong side)

handle

bag (wrong side)

⑥

Sandwich the handle between #⑤ ribbon and the bag. Sew all together.

15cm/ 6 inches

4.5cm/8 inches

101 Bag

1 Sew the bag.
(The same as sewing the lining ⑦ in bag **100**.)

15cm/ 6 inches

outside

Turn 1cm/ 1/2 inch under

Pearl 3mm

2 Turn right side out. Make the fringe on the bottom of the bag, 65 strings. (Refer to Bag #**100** diagram ⑥)

3 Cut velvet ribbon into pieces. (22cm/8 3/4 inches & 30cm/11 3/4 inches, 1 each) Sew trimming to the 30cm /11 3/4 inches piece.

ribbon

(A)

Trimming braid 30cm/11 3/4 inches each

30cm/ 11 3/4 inches

(B)

4 Match the 4mm pearls to the pattern in the trim and sew on.

15cm/6 inches

45cm/17 3/4 inches

14cm/ 1/2 inches

1cm/ 1/2 inch

5 With right sides together, sew the trimmed ribbon on the center seam. Turn right-side out.

14cm/5 1/2 inches

Mini Bag

A bag of beads paired with organdy ribbon.
Used as an accessory, #102 is worn around the neck
and #103 worn diagonally from the shoulder.

102

103

Directions pages 68 & 69

Evening bag

A drawstring bag consisting of an inner bag surrounded by beads
made in the fashion of lariats or necklaces.

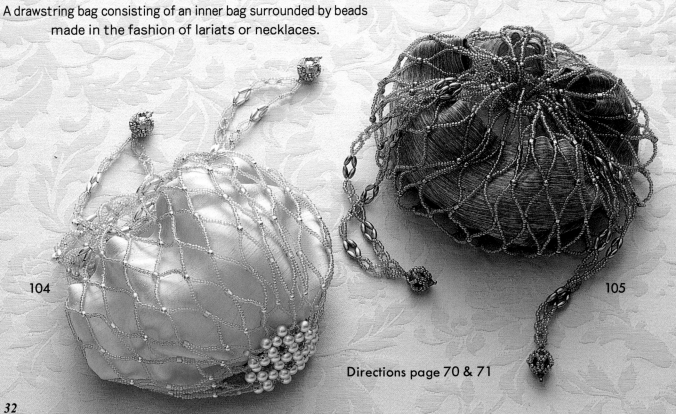

104

105

Directions page 70 & 71

Bag

This handbag and shoulder bag are decorated with the same motif as the choker on page 5.
A lovely design for mature tastes.

106

107

Directions pages 72 & 73

Pouch

A casual bag which goes with anything, can go anywhere at anytime. The focus is the pin from page 22. This one item, the pin, is feminine and so can be enjoyed 2 ways.

108

109

Directions page 74

Amulet bag

This bag made entirely with beads engenders an ethnic feeling. This design is attractive as it can be quickly made using bugle beads.

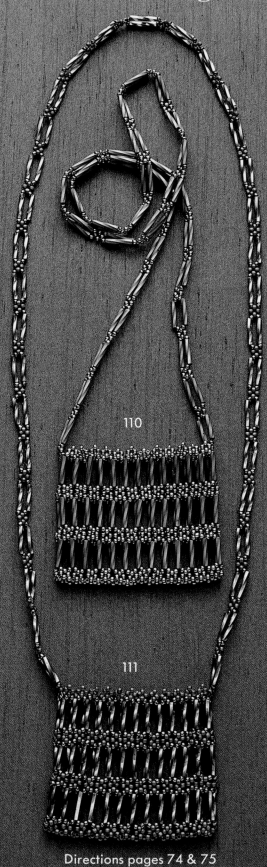

110

111

Directions pages 74 & 75

Bag

These bags become accessories
by the combination of beads.
This is one fashion item which will turn heads.

112

113

114

Directions pages 76 & 77

Beads to Yearn for Total Coordination

115

117

116

Amulet bag, Earring and Ring

A set of accessories grouped around a light pink color scheme. A tiny amulet bag which resembles a pendant and a woven look ring. Swinging earrings which employ bead balls.

Directions page 78 & 79, #117 page 59

Choker, Comb, Earring and Ring

Lovely flower motif accessory set.
A design utilizing chic tones — very practical. For widening your fashion style.

Directions page 80

The butterfly motif of #122 on
the back of the hand, will seem to
dance with each gesture you make.
#123 is to be wrapped double
around the neck, the motif design
laying in the center.
Looks well with open necklines.

122

123

Bracelet, Necklace, Broach and Bag

A mysterious black butterfly motif accessory set.
The butterfly on the bag (#124) is a pin.
Good for one point dressing up of collars, chest, scarf or hat.

124

125

Directions start on page 83～

Choker, Bracelet and Ring

Cute accessory set with small flowers. Three dimensional featuring bugle beads for a form fitting type. #128 bracelet is introduced in an alternative color scheme.

126

127

129

128

Directions page 41, #129 page 45

26 Choker

Materials

Toho Beads / Mill Hill Beads

Small round beads – green (324) 674 beads, white (123) 35 beads, gold (551) 7 beads

3 cut beads – bronze (CR221) 138 beads

Royal bugle beads – 6mm – frosted brown (a-702) 115 beads

Nylon thread – (0.2mm diameter) 540cm/ 212 ½ inches

Colored wire – (0.24mm diameter) silver 90cm/35 ½ inches

Clasp set – bronze 1 set

Craft glue

Directions – String beads on nylon thread to make the foundation. Tidy up the ends and attach the clasp. String beads on wire to make decorations. Use the ends of the wire to attach to the foundation.

Size – 36cm/14 ¼ inches

127 Bracelet

Materials

Toho Beads / Mill Hill Beads

Small round beads – green (324) 254 beads, white (123) 15 beads, gold (551) 3 beads

3 cut beads – bronze (CR221) 66 beads

Royal bugle beads – 6mm – frosted brown (a-702) 45 beads

Nylon thread – (0.2mm diameter) 240cm /94 ½ inches

Colored wire – (0.24mm diameter) silver 60cm/23 ½ inches

Clasp set – bronze 1 set

Craft glue

Directions – Make in the same way as #126 choker

Size – 16cm/6 ¼ inches

128

Materials

Toho Beads / Mill Hill Beads

Small round beads – blue (929) 254 beads, white (123) 15 beads, gold (551a) 3 beads

3 cut beads – bronze (CR 222) 66 beads

Royal bugle beads – 6mm – frosted grey (a-621) 45 beads

Nylon thread – (0.2mm diameter) 240cm /94 ½ inches

Colored wire – (0.24mm diameter) silver 60cm/23 ½ inches

Clasp set – bronze 1 set

Craft glue

Directions – Make in the same way as #126 choker.

Size – 16cm/6 ¼ inches

126 Choker

127·128 Bracelet

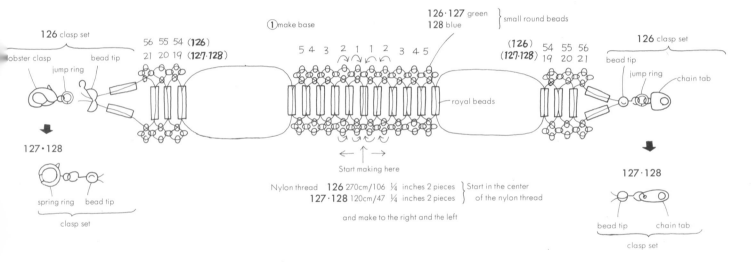

① make base

126·127 green
128 blue } small round beads

56 55 54 **(126)**
21 20 19 **(127·128)**

5 4 3 2 1 1 2 3 4 5

(126)
(127·128) 54 55 56
19 20 21

royal beads

126 clasp set

lobster clasp
jump ring
bead tip

126 clasp set

bead tip
jump ring
chain tab

Start making here

Nylon thread **126** 270cm/106 ¼ inches 2 pieces
127·128 120cm/47 ¼ inches 2 pieces } Start in the center of the nylon thread

and make to the right and the left

127·128

spring ring   bead tip

clasp set

127·128

bead tip   chain tab

clasp set

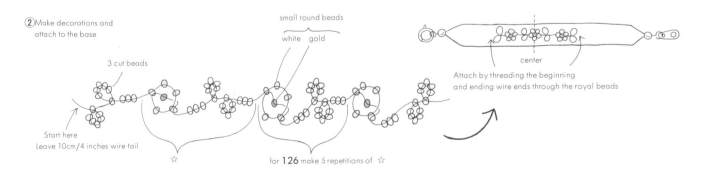

② Make decorations and attach to the base

3 cut beads

small round beads

white   gold

center

Attach by threading the beginning and ending wire ends through the royal beads

Start here
Leave 10cm/4 inches wire tail

☆

for **126** make 5 repetitions of ☆

Directions for #129 ring are on page 45.

5 Lariat

Materials

Toho Beads / Mill Hill Beads

TB beads – bronze (TB-222) 414 beads

Small round beads – light pink (31) 396 beads, red (331) 352 beads, gold (557) 20 beads

Enamel gold Pearl (304/3mm) 2 beads

Frosted gold pearl – (2mm) 2 beads

Faceted glass beads – red (a-5306/ 4 mm) 2 beads

Acrylic beads - orange (a-202/12mm) 2 beads

Bead cap – antique bronze 4 beads

Nylon thread – (0.2mm diameter) 380cm/ 149 ½ inches

Craft glue

Directions – Thread beads onto nylon thread to make bead ball. Thread beads and bead ball on nylon thread to make 2 lariats. Attach the 2 lariats and tidy up the ends.

Size – 85cm/33 ½ inches

6

Material

Toho Beads / Mill Hill Beads

Small round beads – bronze (221) 288 beads, white (147) 254 beads, gold (557) 214 beads, amber (2) 20 beads

Enamel gold pearl (304/3mm) 2 beads

Crystal cut beads – topaz (J-54/4mm/ #3) 4 beads

Acrylic beads - white (a-225) 12mm – 1 bead, 8mm – 1 bead

Nylon thread – (0.2mm diameter) 310cm/ 122 inches

Craft glue

Directions – Thread beads on nylon thread to form 2 bead balls. (Make one the same as the earring #68 on page 59) Thread beads and bead balls on nylon thread and make 2 lariats. Make an opening for one end of the lariat part way through one side. Attach the 2 lariats and tidy up the ends.

Size – 36cm/14 ¼ inches (Full length 54cm/21 ¼ inches)

5·6 small round beads, unless stated otherwise

Making the bead ball

Tie firmly and glue to secure at one point

Start
Nylon thread 40cm
/15 ¾ inches
leave 5cm/2 inches
at the end

5·6 gold
5 TB beads 6 bronze
5 red 6 amber
5 light pink 6 white
thread through ☆
☆ →
★ →
thread through ★

place acrylic bead
in the center before closing

make 2 for 5 and 1 for 6
(Make 1 more bead ball for #6
the same as for #68 earring on page 59)

acrylic bead

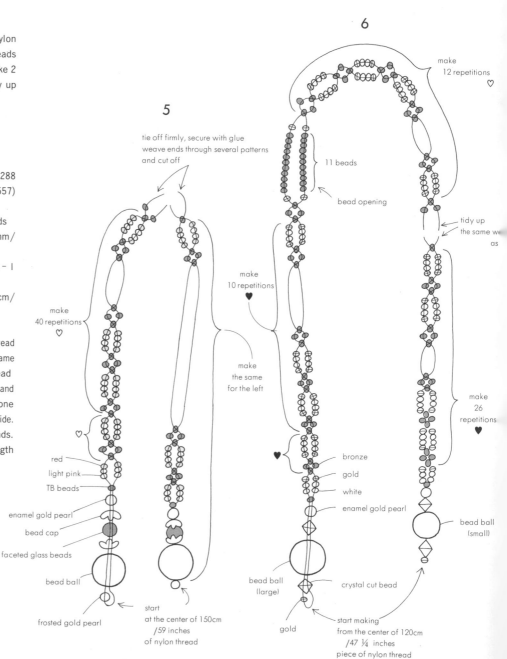

5

tie off firmly, secure with glue
weave ends through several patterns
and cut off

make
40 repetitions
♡

♡

red
light pink
TB beads

enamel gold pearl
bead cap
faceted glass beads
bead ball

frosted gold pearl

start
at the center of 150cm
/59 inches
of nylon thread

bead ball
(large)

gold

6

make
12 repetitions
♡

11 beads

bead opening

make
10 repetitions
♥

make
the same
for the left

♥

bronze
gold
white
enamel gold pearl

crystal cut bead

tidy up
the same w
as

make
26
repetitions
♥

bead ball
(small)

start making
from the center of 120cm
/47 ¼ inches
piece of nylon thread

7 Lariat

Materials

Toho Beads / Mill Hill Beads

Small round beads – pink (11) 1703 beads, metallic pink (9556) 720 beads, clear frosted gold (262) 504 beads, metallic gold (204) 408 beads

Decora beads – orange (a-5605) 2 beads

Beading thread – white (100m spool) 1

Directions – Thread beads on string to make tassel. With another thread pick up the tassel, continue making 2 lariats. Join together.

Size – 100cm/39 ½ inches

8

Materials

Toho Beads / Mill Hill Beads

Small round beads – amber (2) 2087 beads, bronze (221) 744 beads, green (246) 504 beads

Decora beads – beige (a-5609) 2 beads

Beading thread – white (100m spool) 1

Directions – Make the same as for lariat 8.

Size – 100cm/39 ½ inches

9

Materials

Toho Beads / Mill Hill Beads

Small round beads – white (147) 1703 beads, green (946) 720 beads, salmon pink (923) 504 beads, gold (557) 384 beads

Frosted gold pearl – (2mm) 24 beads

Decora beads – white (a-5603) 2 beads

Beading thread – white (100m spool) 1

Directions – Make the same as for lariat 7.

Size – 100cm/39 ½ inches

7•8•9

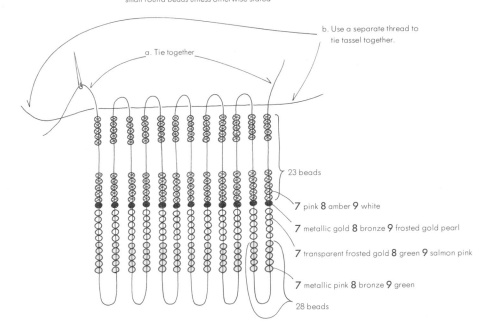

small round beads unless otherwise stated

a. Tie together

b. Use a separate thread to tie tassel together.

23 beads

7 pink 8 amber 9 white

7 metallic gold 8 bronze 9 frosted gold pearl

7 transparent frosted gold 8 green 9 salmon pink

7 metallic pink 8 bronze 9 green

28 beads

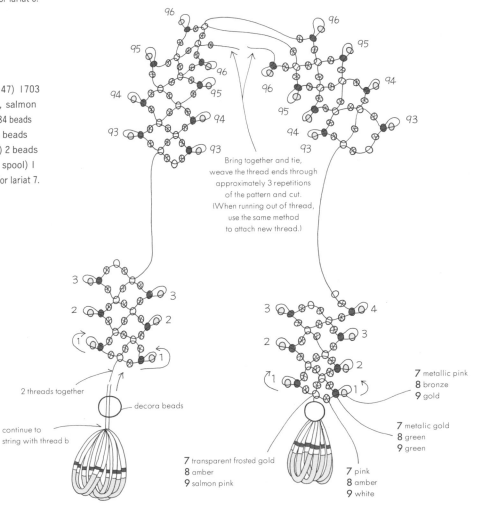

Bring together and tie, weave the thread ends through approximately 3 repetitions of the pattern and cut. (When running out of thread, use the same method to attach new thread.)

2 threads together

decora beads

continue to string with thread b

7 metallic pink
8 bronze
9 gold

7 metalic gold
8 green
9 green

7 transparent frosted gold
8 amber
9 salmon pink

7 pink
8 amber
9 white

PAGE 5

10 Choker

Materials

Toho Beads / Mill Hill Beads

Small round beads – green (324) 284 beads, blue (952) 166 beads

Bugle beads – 6mm – bronze (221) 72 beads

Colored wire – (0.24mm diameter) gold 150cm/59 inches

Ribbon – dark brown (3mm width) 150cm /59 inches

Directions – Thread the beads on the colored wire. Attach ribbon.

Size – 95cm – 37 ½ inches

Materials

Toho Beads / Mill Hill Beads

Small round beads – blue (243) 284 beads, salmon pink (955) 166 beads

Bugle beads – 6mm – bronze (222) 72 beads

Colored wire – (0.24mm diameter) gold 150cm/59 inches

Ribbon – grey (5mm width) 150cm/59 inches

Directions – Make the same as for choker #10.

Size – 95cm/37 ½ inches

10·11

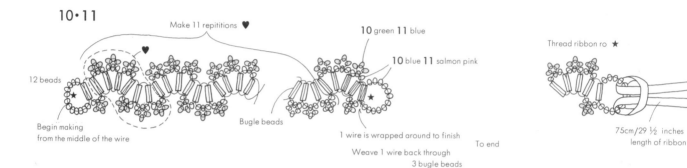

Make 11 repititions ♥

12 beads

Begin making
from the middle of the wire

Bugle beads

10 green 11 blue

10 blue 11 salmon pink

1 wire is wrapped around to finish

Weave 1 wire back through
3 bugle beads

To end

Thread ribbon ro ★

75cm/29 ½ inches
length of ribbon

12 Choker

Materials

Toho Beads / Mill Hill Beads

Small round beads – salmon pink (955) 300 beads, green (324) 296 beads, bronze (221) 228 beads

Nylon thread – (0.2mm diameter) 280cm/ 110 ¼ inches

Ribbon – golden brown (3mm width) 150cm /59 inches

Craft glue

Directions – Start stringing beads from the middle and work right and left.
Thread ribbon through the star marks at the ends and tie.

Size – 26cm/10 ¼ inches long (excluding the ribbon)

12

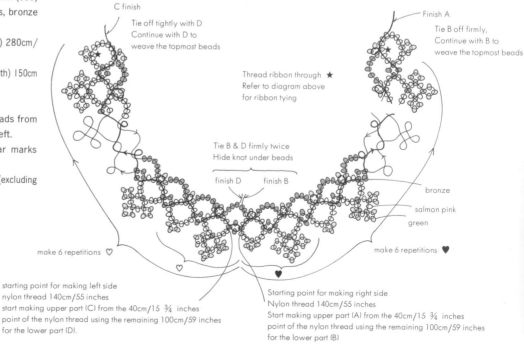

C finish
Tie off tightly with D
Continue with D to
weave the topmost beads

Finish A
Tie B off firmly,
Continue with B to
weave the topmost beads

Thread ribbon through ★
Refer to diagram above
for ribbon tying

Tie B & D firmly twice
Hide knot under beads

finish D   finish B

bronze
salmon pink
green

make 6 repetitions ♡

make 6 repetitions ♥

starting point for making left side
nylon thread 140cm/55 inches
start making upper part (C) from the 40cm/15 ¾ inches
point of the nylon thread using the remaining 100cm/59 inches
for the lower part (D).

Starting point for making right side
Nylon thread 140cm/55 inches
Start making upper part (A) from the 40cm/15 ¾ inches
point of the nylon thread using the remaining 100cm/59 inches
for the lower part (B)

13

Materials

Toho Beads / Mill Hill Beads

Small round beads – blue metallic (81) 204 beads, purple (115) 196 beads, light purple (6) 195 beads, dusty lavendar (267) 180 beads grey (266) 96 beads, bronze (222) 98 beads

Nylon thread – (0.2mm diameter) 280cm/ 110 ¼ inches

Ribbon – purple (6mm width) 95cm/37 ½ inches

Craft glue

Directions – Make as for #12 choker.

Size – 26cm/10 ¼ inches long (excluding the ribbon)

14

Materials

Toho Beads / Mill Hill Beads

Small round beads – blue (953) 387 beads, gold (22) 208 beads, bronze (221) 194 beads, amber (2) 180 beads

Nylon thread – (0.2mm diameter) 280cm /110 ¼ inches

Ribbon – golden brown (3mm width) 150 cm/59 Pinches

Craft glue

Directions – Make as for #12 choker.

Size – 26cm/10 ¼ inches long (excluding the ribbon)

Color Scheme Chart

	13 purple tone	14 blue tone
O	bronze	bronze
O	light purple	blue
●	purple	gold
◐	blue metallic	gold
◑	purple	blue
◎	blue metallic	blue
O	dusty lavendar	amber
�◉	grey	bronze

13・14

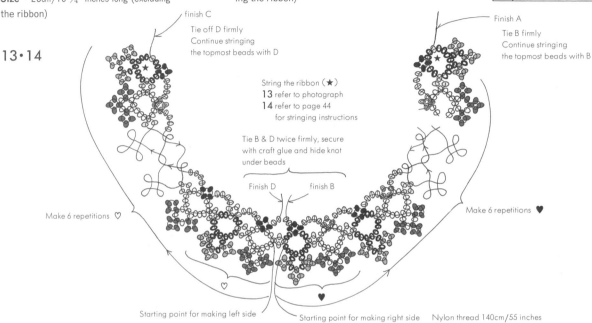

finish C
Tie off D firmly
Continue stringing
the topmost beads with D

Finish A
Tie B firmly
Continue stringing
the topmost beads with B

String the ribbon (★)
13 refer to photograph
14 refer to page 44
for stringing instructions

Tie B & D twice firmly, secure with craft glue and hide knot under beads

Finish D   finish B

Make 6 repetitions ♡

Make 6 repetitions ♥

Starting point for making left side
Nylon thread 140cm/55 inches
start making upper part (C) from the 40cm/15 ¾ inches
point of the nylon thread using the remaining
100cm/59 inches for the lower part (D)

Starting point for making right side

Nylon thread 140cm/55 inches
Start making upper part (A) from the 40cm
point of the nylon thread using the remaining
100cm for the lower part (B)

29

PAGE 40

Ring

Materials

Toho Beads / Mill Hill Beads

Small round beads – green (324) 120 beads, white (123) 5 beads, gold (551) 1 bead

3 cut beads (6mm) – bronze (CR221) 19 beads

Royal bugle beads – frosted brown (a–702) 20 beads

Nylon thread – (0.2mm diameter) 100cm /59 inches

Colored wire – (0.24mm diameter) silver 40cm/15 ¾ inches

Craft glue

Directions – String beads on nylon thread to make foundation. Tie the beginning and end together to make a loop and tidy up the ends. String beads on wire to make decorations. Use ends of wires to tie the decorations to the foundation.

Size – Interior diameter 5.5cm/2 ¼ inches.

1. Make foundation

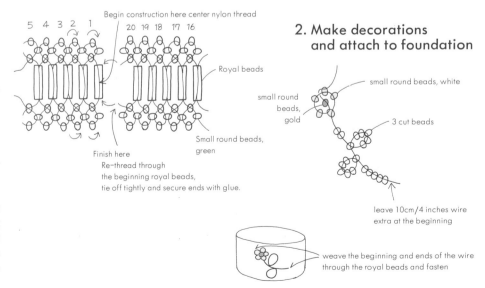

Begin construction here center nylon thread

5 4 3 2 1   20 19 18 17 16

Royal beads

Small round beads, green

Finish here
Re–thread through
the beginning royal beads,
tie off tightly and secure ends with glue.

2. Make decorations and attach to foundation

small round beads, white

small round beads, gold

3 cut beads

leave 10cm/4 inches wire extra at the beginning

weave the beginning and ends of the wire through the royal beads and fasten

15 Necklace

Materials

Toho Beads / Mill Hill Beads

TB beads – off white (TB-123) 1700 beads, brownish green (TB-262) 1526 beads

Decora beads – clear yellow (a-5606) 4 beads, white (a-5610) 3 beads, white (a-5607) 2 beads

Bead caps (large) – antique gold 10 beads

Bead caps (small) – antique gold 8 beads

Beading thread – white 13m

Clasp set – bronze 1 set

Craft glue

Directions – String beads on thread. Separate into 2 groups of 5 strands each and twist each group. Finish up the ends. Attach clasp. To wear, twist all together and hook clasp.

Size – 41cm

16

Materials

TB beads – black (TB-49) 1700 beads, brown (TB-423) 1056 beads, pink (TB-741) 481 beads

Decora beads – clear orange (a-5612) 3 beads, clear orange (a-5605) 2 beads, clear orange (a-5608) 2 beads

Bead cap (large) – antique bronze 10 beads

Bead cap (small) – antique bronze 4 beads

Beading thread – white 13m

Clasp set – bronze 1 set

Craft glue

Directions – Make as for #15 necklace.

Size – 41cm/16 ¼ inches

15

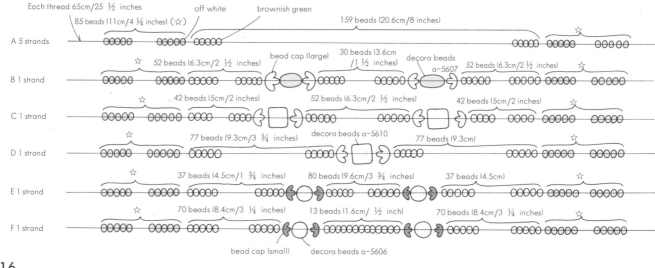

16

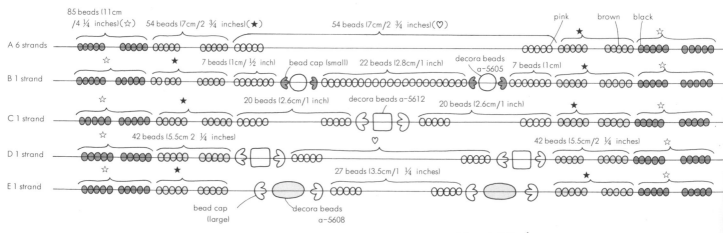

17 PAGE 7
Necklace

Materials

Toho Beads / Mill Hill Beads

TB beads – clear purple (TB-6F), brown (TB-114), crystal grey (TB-176), light salmon pink (TB-763), and pink (TB-764) 646 beads each

Beading thread – white 12m

Clasp set – bronze 1 set

Craft glue

Directions – String beads on thread. Separate into 2 groups of 5 each and twist each together. Tidy up ends and attach claps. To wear, twist the whole again and close the clasp.

Size – 42cm/16 ½ inches

18 Bracelet

Materials

Toho Beads / Mill Hill Beads

TB beads – clear purple (TB-6F), brown (TB-114), crystal grey (TB-176), light salmon pink (TB-763), and pink (TB-764) 278 beads each

Beading thread – white 800cm/315 inches

Clasp set – bronze 1 set

Craft glue

Directions – Make as for #17 necklace

Size – 18cm/7 inches

17 necklace 18 bracelet

String beads on doubled thread (Make 2 of each color)

Necklace 323 beads (42cm/116 ½ inches)
Bracelet 139 beads (18cm/7 inches)

TB beads

Thread   Necklace 60cm/23 ½ inches
Bracelet 40cm/15 ¾ inches

17

spring ring

tie the thread ends, secure with craft glue and close bead tip over

chain tab

bead tip

Make 2 groups with one of each color. Twist each group to make 2 groups.

Twist the 2 together in the opposite direction

18

lobster clasp

chain tab

bead tip

※spring ring (lobster clasp) chain tab, bead tip are included in one clasp set

19 PAGE 8
Necklace

Materials

Toho Beads / Mill Hill Beads

Maga tama beads – transparent pink (171/4mm) 85 beads

Acrylic cut beads – black (a-352/6mm) 7 beads

Beading wire – moss green (1mm diameter) 50cm/19 ¾ inches

Eye pins – antique gold (30mm) 18 pins

Jump ring – antique gold (3.8mm round) 25 pieces

Clasp set – bronze 1 set

Directions – String beads and eye pins as shown. Connect with jump rings.

Size – 42cm/16 ½ inches long

20

Materials

Toho Beads / Mill Hill Beads

Acrylic cut beads – black (a-352/6mm) 6 beads, grey blue (a-269/8mm) 1 bead

Maga tama beads – transparent (M01/4mm) 5 beads

3 cut beads – black (CR 49) 8 beads

Beading wire – bronze (1mm diameter) 50cm/19 ¾ inches

Cable chain – bronze (8mm) 40cm/15 ¾ inches

Eye pin – antique gold (30mm) 4 pins

Jump rings – antique gold (3.8mm round) 9 pieces

Clasp set – bronze 1 set

Directions – Make the parts and connect with jump rings.

Size – Refer to diagram.

20

Same as #19

Jump ring
Clasp set

Cut cable chain in half, fold in half for each side

10cm/4 inches

eye pin

acrylic cut beads 8mm

eye pin

jump ring

eye pin

acrylic cut beads 6mm

3 cut beads

maga tama beads

eye pin

use pliers to bend art wire (same as for 19)

13cm/5 inches

19

spring ring   chain tab (small)

clasp set

make 3 repetitions ♥

8 beads

acrylic cut beads

eye pin

beading wire

1.5cm

after bending with pliers, open to the right and the left(same as for 20)

eye pin

jump ring

maga tama beads

eye pin

2.2cm

21 Necklace

Materials

Toho Beads / Mill Hill Beads

Maga tama beads − red (M45), red & transparent (M105) 4mm 12 beads each, transparent (01) 8 beads

Stone charms − carnelian 1 piece

Beading wire − silver (0.75mm diameter) 15cm/6 inches

Accessory cord − black (0.4mm diameter/ with 4 crimp tubes) 45cm

Crimp tubes − silver 10 pieces

Clasp set − bronze 1 set

Jump rings − silver (3.8mm round) 2 pieces

Directions − Thread the stone charms in the middle of the accessory cord, then beads to the right and left.

Size − 42.5cm/16 ¾ inches

23 Necklace

Materials

Toho Beads / Mill Hill Beads

3 cut beads − pinkish gold (CR509) 126 pieces

Twisted bugle beads − pinkish gold (CR514/ 12mm) 7 beads

Metal parts, joint − bronze 8 pieces

Accessory cord − silver (0.4mm diameter /with 4 crimp tubes) 60cm/23 ½ inches

Eye pin − antique silver (30mm) 7 pins

Jump rings − antique silver (3.8mm round) 14 pieces

Clasp set − bronze 1 set

Directions − Thread twisted bugle beads on eye pins, connect parts with jump rings and then connect beads.

Size − 42.5cm/16 ¾ inches

24

Materials

Toho Beads / Mill Hill Beads

3 cut beads − black (CR49) 126 beads

Twisted bugle beads − bronze (221/12 mm) 7 beads

Metal parts, joint − gold 8 pieces

Accessory cord − gold (0.4mm diameter /with4 crimp tubes) 60cm/23 ½ inches

Eye pins − antique gold (30mm) 7 pins

Jump rings − antique silver (3.8mm round) 14 pieces

Clasp set − bronze 1 set

Directions − Make as for necklace #23.

Size − 42.5cm/16 ¾ inches

22

Materials

Toho Beads / Mill Hill Beads

Maga tama beads − transparent (M21), blue purple × transparent (M348) 4mm 16 beads each

Stone charms − lavendar amethyst 1 piece

Beading wire − silver (0.75mm diameter) 15cm/6 inches

Accessory cord − black (0.4mm diameter/ with 4 crimp tubes) 45cm/17 ¾ inches

Crimp tubes − silver 10 pieces

Clasp set − bronze 1 set

Jump rings − silver (3.8mm round) 2 pieces

Directions − Make as for necklace #21.

Size − 42.5cm/16 ¾ inches

21·22

spring ring
chain tab (small) } clasp set
bead tip

String the end of the accessory cord through the bead tip.   Use the attached crimp tube to secure cord.

11.5cm/4 ½ inches

22 color scheme

crimp tube
red
red and transparent } maga tama beads 4mm
transparent

transparent
blue purple and transparent } maga tama beads 4mm

2cm/ ¾ inch

2cm/ ¾ inch

stone charms
21 carnelian, 22 lavendar amethyst

attach with a jump ring for the bottom wire to face full front

bend wire with pliers

2cm

25

Materials

Toho Beads / Mill Hill Beads

Royal beads, 3 cut − silver (CR713) 126 beads

Twisted bugle beads − yellowish green (721/12mm) 7 beads

Metal parts, joint − silver 8 pieces

Accessory cord − silver (0.4mm diameter /with 4 crimp tubes) 60cm/23 ½ inches

Eye pins − antique silver (30mm) 7 pins

Jump rings − antique silver (3.8mm round) 14 pieces

Clasp set − bronze 1 set

Directions − Make as for #23 necklace.

Size − 42.5cm/16 ¾ inches long

23·24·25

clasp set
lobster clasp   chain tab (large)

crimp tube

63 beads

9cm/ 3 ½ inches

23·24 3 cut beads
25 royal beads 3 cut

accessory cord

crimp tubes

eye pin

twisted bugle beads

jump ring

metal parts, joint

26 PAGE 9
Necklace

Materials

Toho Beads / Mill Hill Beads

3 cut beads – off white (CR122) 312 beads

Maga tama beads – amber (M22/4mm) 42 beads

Nylon thread – (0.3mm diameter) 360cm /141 ¾ inches

Crimp tubes (small) – antique bronze 2 pieces

Clasp set – bronze 1 set

Directions – Prepare 6 strands of nylon thread, 60cm/23 ½ inches each. Construct from ends. Taping the ends of the nylon thread down to anchor makes for easy construction.

Size – 41cm/161 ½ inches

27
Materials

Toho Beads / Mill Hill Beads

3 cut beads – bronze (CR221) 312 beads

Maga tama beads – amber (M22/4mm) 42 beads

Nylon thread – (0.3mm diameter) 360cm/ 141 ¾ inches

Crimp tubes (small) – antique bronze 2 pieces

Clasp set – bronze 1 set

Directions – Make as for #26 necklace.

Size – 41cm/16 ½ inches

26・27

spring ring
bead tip
chain tab (small)
clasp set

clasp set
bead tip

secure with crimp tubes in the clasp set and put inside of bead tip

make 9.5 repetitions ♥

Maga tama beads 4mm

3 cut beads

middle

28 PAGE 10
Pendant

Materials

Toho Beads / Mill Hill Beads

Small round beads – bronze (556) 69 beads, white (147) 15 beads, pink (151) 15 beads, amber (2) 15 beads, metallic gold (557) 1 bead

3 cut beads – bronze (CR222) 114 beads

Colored pearl – bronze (3mm) 74 beads

Acrylic cut beads – wine (a-266/6mm) 7 beads

Rose beads – gold (a-2357/6mm) 2 beads

Bead cap – antique bronze 14 pieces

Eye pins – antique bronze 49 pins

Colored wire – (0.24mm diameter) silver 150cm/59 inches

Clasp set – antique bronze 1 set

Directions – Make the ring and the flowers. Attach flowers to ring with wire. Thread beads on eye pins and then put together.

Size – 42cm/16 ½ inches

· Make the same for both unless otherwise indicated
· pull wire tightly while making

ring 28 bronze 74 black 75 metallic pink

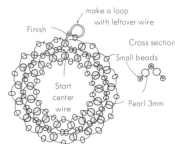

make a loop with leftover wire

Finish

Cross section

Small beads

Start center wire

Pearl 3mm

clasp set

spring ring   chain tab   jump ring

28

same as other side

rose beads

pearl 3mm

eye pin

acrylic cut bead

bead cap

attach with eye pin

attach flower ring with wire

Flower ring wire 70cm/27 ½ inches (start in the center of the wire)

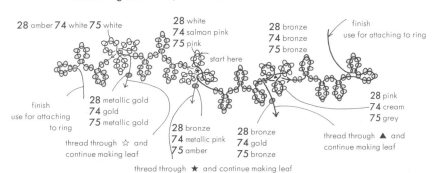

28 amber 74 white 75 white

28 white 74 salmon pink 75 pink

28 bronze 74 bronze 75 bronze

finish use for attaching to ring

start here

28 pink 74 cream 75 grey

finish use for attaching to ring

28 metallic gold 74 gold 75 metallic gold

28 bronze 74 metallic pink 75 amber

thread through ☆ and continue making leaf

28 bronze 74 gold 75 bronze

thread through ▲ and continue making leaf

thread through ★ and continue making leaf

Materials

Toho Beads / Mill Hill Beads

Small round beads – light pink (151) 900 beads, dark pink (201) 179 beads, metallic pink (556) 76 beads, grey (112) 28 beads

TB beads – bronze (TB-222) 76 beads

Frosted pearl – gold (2mm) 23 beads

Crystal cut beads – amethyst (J-54/4mm/#8) 10 beads

Faceted glass beads – amethyst (a-5308/4mm) 2 beads

Large round pearl – enamel gold (5mm) 1 bead

King sized beads – frosted pink (6F/5.5mm) 1 bead

Semi-precious beads – fancy agate (a-1541/4mm) 1 bead

Rose beads – gold (a-2357/6mm) 1 bead

Bead cap (small) – antique bronze 4 pieces

Nylon thread – (0.2mm diameter) 310cm/122 inches

Colored wire – (0.24mm diameter) silver 100cm/39 ½ inches

Craft glue

Perfume bottle – bottom diameter 1.4cm / ½ inch, height 3.5cm/1 ½ inches

Directions – When partly made, insert perfume bottle and pull the nylon thread continuing to make the body. Make the necklace with nylon thread. Make the flowers from wire and attach.

Size – 61cm/24 inches

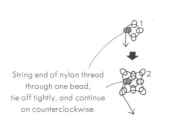

String end of nylon thread through one bead, tie off tightly, and continue on counterclockwise.

Making the bottle cover

Nylon thread 150cm/59 inches

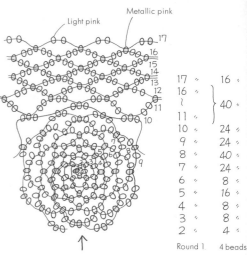

Light pink
Metallic pink

Insert bottle at approximately the 9th round and pull the nylon thread tightly while continuing to construct

17 "	16 "	
16 "		
↕	}	40 "
11 "		
10 "	24 "	
9 "	24 "	
8 "	40 "	
7 "	24 "	
6 "	8 "	
5 "	16 "	
4 "	8 "	
3 "	8 "	
2 "	4 "	
Round 1	4 beads	

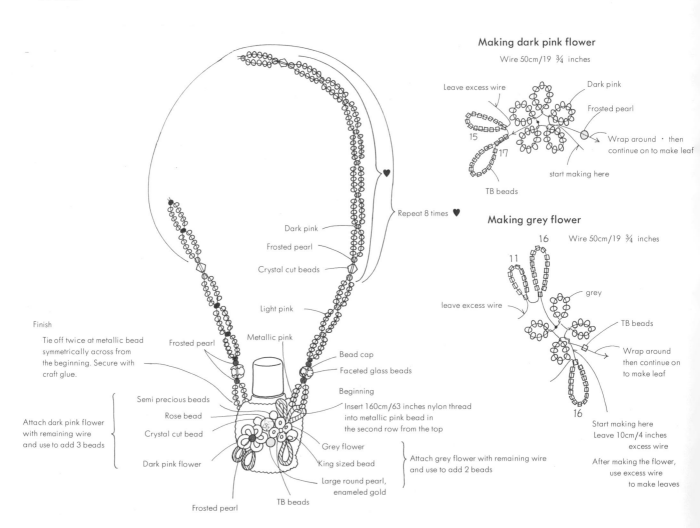

Dark pink
Frosted pearl
Crystal cut beads
Light pink
Metallic pink

Repeat 8 times ♥

Finish

Tie off twice at metallic bead symmetrically across from the beginning. Secure with craft glue.

Attach dark pink flower with remaining wire and use to add 3 beads

Frosted pearl
Semi precious beads
Rose bead
Crystal cut bead
Dark pink flower

Frosted pearl
TB beads

Bead cap
Faceted glass beads

Beginning

Insert 160cm/63 inches nylon thread into metallic pink bead in the second row from the top

Grey flower
King sized bead
Large round pearl, enameled gold

Attach grey flower with remaining wire and use to add 2 beads

Making dark pink flower

Wire 50cm/19 ¾ inches

Leave excess wire
Dark pink
Frosted pearl
Wrap around · then continue on to make leaf
start making here
TB beads

Making grey flower

Wire 50cm/19 ¾ inches

leave excess wire
grey
TB beads
Wrap around then continue on to make leaf

Start making here Leave 10cm/4 inches excess wire

After making the flower, use excess wire to make leaves

PAGE 11
30 Pendant

Materials

Toho Beads / Mill Hill Beads

Small round beads – black (49) 120 beads, bronze (221) 1 bead

TB beads – green (TB422) 77 beads, cream (TB-162) 56 beads

Black pearl – 3mm – 42 beads, 4mm – 37 beads

Faceted glass beads – topaz (a–5304/4mm) 4 beads

Bead cap (large) – antique gold 1 piece

Bead cap (small) – antique gold 8 pieces

Eye pin – antique gold (30mm) 41 pieces

Jump rings – antique gold (3.8mm round) 6 pieces

Cable chain – antique gold (40cm) 1

Metal parts, joint– antique gold 1 piece

Nylon thread – (0.2mm diameter) 120cm/47 ¼ inches

Colored wire – (0.23mm diameter) gold 60cm/23 ½ inches

Clasp set – antique gold 1 set

Craft glue

Directions – Make the cross with nylon thread. Continue by making the flowers and attaching. Make chain by threading beads on eye pins and putting together.

Size – 44cm/17 ¼ inches

31

Materials

Toho Beads / Mill Hill Beads

Small round beads – gun metal (81) 120 beads, bronze (222) 1 bead

TB beads – bronze (TB-221) 77 beads, pink (TB-741) 56 beads

Round pearl – dark gun metal 3mm – 42 beads, 4mm – 37 beads

Faceted glass beads – light orange (a–5307/4mm) 4 beads

Bead caps – (large) antique bronze 1 piece

Bead caps – (small) antique bronze 8 pieces

Eye pins – antique bronze (30mm) 41 pins

Jump rings – antique bronze (3.8mm round) 6 pieces

Cable chain – antique bronze (40cm) 1 chain

Metal parts, joint – antique bronze 1 piece

Nylon thread – (0.2mm diameter) 120cm/47 ¼ inches

Colored wire – (0.23mm diameter) gold 60cm

Clasp set – antique bronze 1 set

Craft glue

Directions – Make as for pendant #30.

Size – 44cm/17 ¼ inches

Making the flower   Wire 60cm/23 ½ inches

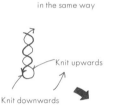

TB beads
30 green
31 bronze

TB beads
30 cream
31 pink

small round beads
30 bronze
31 bronze

finish
use the remaining wire to attach to the cross (do the other one the same way)

Start here (☆)

30·31   Making the cross

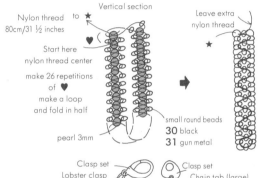

Vertical section

Nylon thread to ★
80cm/31 ½ inches

Start here
nylon thread center

make 26 repetitions
of ♥
make a loop
and fold in half

pearl 3mm

small round beads
30 black
31 gun metal

(side view)

Leave extra nylon thread

★

Continue adding beads while closing the hole Close the other side in the same way

Knit upwards

Knit downwards

horizontal length

Start here
Nylon thread
40cm/15 ¾ inches

String through the small round beads on the other side and close the sides as done for the vertical length.

Jump ring

Bead cap

String the leftover nylon thread through the bead cap and jump ring, beads. Tie off tightly twice at the edge of the bead and secure with glue.

Make as for the left side

String 60cm/23 ½ inches wire through to make flower (☆)

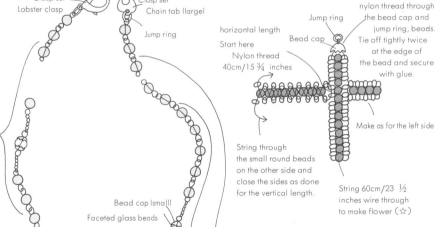

Clasp set
Lobster clasp

Clasp set
Chain tab (large)

Jump ring

Make 2 repetitions
♥

Bead cap (small)

Faceted glass beads

Cable chain
5 beads

Eye pin

Metal parts, joint

Jump ring

Pearl bead 4mm

Make 2 repetitions ♥

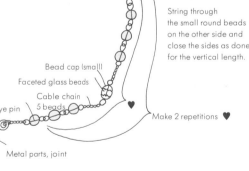

51

32 Choker

Materials

Toho Beads / Mill Hill Beads

Maga tama beads – amber (M22/4mm) 8 beads

TB beads – goldish (TB-262) 554 beads, grey (TB-112) & pink (TB-741) 150 beads each, cream (TB-948) 100 beads

Colored wire – (0.35~0.37mm diameter) gold 200cm/78 ¾ inches

Accessory cord – gold (0.4mm/with 4 crimp tubes) 1 set

Clasp set – antique gold 1 set

Directions – Thread beads on wire. Thread accessory cord through the last leaf, secure with crimp tube and string beads. Tidy up with bead tip and crimp tubes from the clasp set and attach spring ring and chain tab with jump rings.

Size – 35cm/13 ¾ inches

33

Materials

Toho Beads / Mill Hill Beads

Maga tama beads – amber (M22. 4mm) 8 beads

TB beads – bronze (TB-222) 302 beads, blue (TB-7BD) & purple (TB-166) 150 beads each, amber (TB-162) 100 beads

Colored wire – (0.35~0.37mm diameter) gold 200cm/78 ¾ inches

Cable chain – (with spring ring, chain tab and jump ring included) bronze 1 set

Directions – String beads on wire. Attach chain to last leaf with jump ring. Attach spring ring and chain tab to chain with jump rings.

Size – 37cm/14 ½ inches

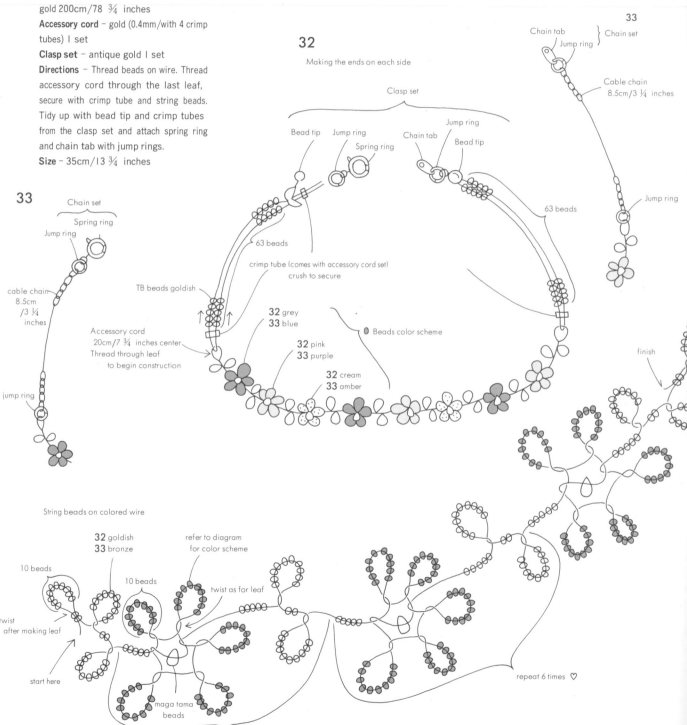

32

Making the ends on each side

Clasp set

Bead tip   Jump ring

Spring ring

Chain tab   Jump ring

Bead tip

63 beads

63 beads

crimp tube (comes with accessory cord set) crush to secure

TB beads goldish

32 grey
33 blue

32 pink
33 purple

32 cream
33 amber

Beads color scheme

Accessory cord 20cm/7 ¾ inches center Thread through leaf to begin construction

33

Chain set

Spring ring

Jump ring

cable chain 8.5cm /3 ¼ inches

jump ring

33

Chain tab   Chain set

Jump ring

Cable chain 8.5cm/3 ¼ inches

Jump ring

finish

String beads on colored wire

32 goldish
33 bronze

refer to diagram for color scheme

10 beads

10 beads

twist as for leaf

twist after making leaf

start here

maga tama beads

repeat 6 times ♡

♡

37 Ring

PAGE 14

Materials

Toho Beads / Mill Hill Beads

Small round beads – gold (22) 67 beads, metallic gold (557) 5 beads, white (123) 1 bead

Round pearl – ivory (3mm) 35 beads

Half pearl – ivory (10mm) 1 bead

Nylon thread – (0.2mm diameter) 90cm/ 35 ½ inches

Craft glue

Directions – Make as for #38 ring

Size – Interior diameter 5.5cm/2 ¼ inches

38

Materials

Toho Beads / Mill Hill Beads

Small round beads – bronze (222) 72 beads, light pink (556) 1 bead

Colored pearls – bronze (3mm) 35 beads

Half pearl – ivory (10mm) 1 bead

Nylon thread – (0.2mm diameter) 90cm/ 35 ½ inches

Craft glue

Directions – String beads on nylon thread. After making the front, turn to the back and add more beads. Before closing insert half pearl. Continue to make the ring. Pull the ends of the nylon thread tightly and tie. Secure with craft glue.

Size – Interior diameter 5.5cm/2 ¼ inches

39

Materials

Toho Beads / Mill Hill Beads

Small round beads – bronze (222) 72 beads

Round pearl – dark gun metal (3mm) 35 beads, gun metal (2mm) 1 bead

Half pearl – ivory (10mm) 1 bead

Nylon thread – (0.2mm diameter) 90cm/ 35 ½ inches

Craft glue

Directions – Make as for #38 ring.

Size – Interior diameter 5.metal (203/3mm) 35 beads, gun metal (202/2mm) 1 bead Half pearl – 5cm/2 ¼ inches.

37·38·39 small round beads unless otherwise indicated

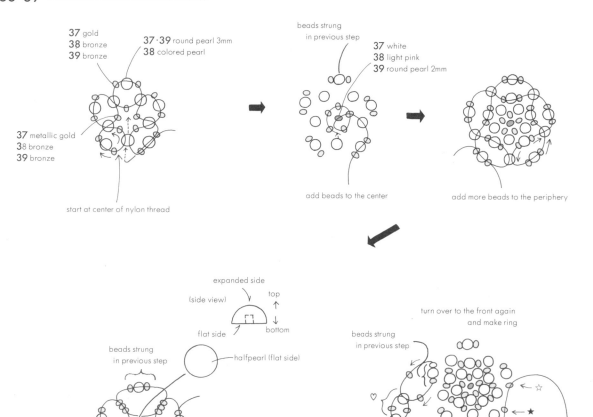

37 gold
38 bronze
39 bronze

37·39 round pearl 3mm
38 colored pearl

37 metallic gold
38 bronze
39 bronze

start at center of nylon thread

beads strung in previous step

37 white
38 light pink
39 round pearl 2mm

add beads to the center

add more beads to the periphery

expanded side
(side view)
top
flat side
bottom

beads strung in previous step

halfpearl (flat side)

☆
★

turn to the back and add beads before fully closing insert half pearl

turn over to the front again and make ring

beads strung in previous step

☆
★

tie off tightly and secure with craft glue

make 14 repetitions
♡

40 Ring

Materials

Toho Beads / Mill Hill Beads

3 cut beads – pinkish (CR509) 34 beads

Hexagon beads – bronze (221/small) 12 beads

Bugle beads (3mm) – bronze (221) 16 beads

Bugle beads (6mm) – bronze (221) 4 beads

Round pearl – gold enamel (3mm) 2 beads

Retro beads – antique gold (a-360) 1 bead

Joint – antique gold 2 pieces

Bead cap – antique silver 2 pieces

Nylon thread – (0.2mm diameter) 60cm/ 23 ½ inches

Craft glue

Directions – String beads on nylon thread and make a loop. When round 1 is finished, make round 2 underneath. Tie off nylon thread tightly and secure with craft glue.

Size – Interior diameter 5.5cm

41

Materials

Toho Beads / Mill Hill Beads

3 cut beads – silver (CR711) 34 beads

Hexagon beads – gun metal (81/small) 12 beads

Bugle beads (3mm) – gun metal (81) 16 beads

Bugle beads (6mm) – gun metal (81) 4 beads

Round pearl – gun metal (3mm) 2 beads

Retro beads – antique silver (a-359) 1 bead

Joint – antique gold 2 beads

Bead cap – antique gold 2 pieces

Nylon thread – (0.2mm diameter) 60cm/ 23 ½ inches

Craft glue

Directions – Make as for #40 ring.

Size – Interior diameter 5.5cm/2 ¼ inches

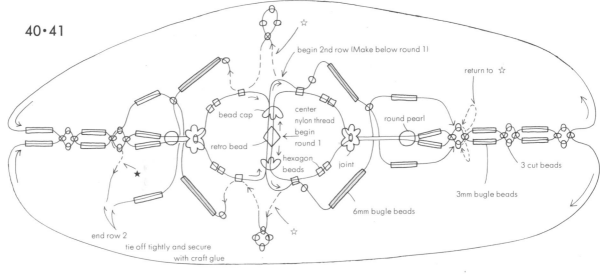

40·41

42 Ring

Materials

Toho Beads / Mill Hill Beads

TB beads – cream (TB-162) 168 beads, blue (TB-932) 70 beads, red (TB-5) 25 beads, metallic (TB-422) 53 beads, green (TB-940) 24 beads, brown (TB-951) 2 beads, light blue (TB-23) 13 beads, dark pink (TB-332) 6 beads, pink (TB-241) 46 beads, yellow (TB-949) 13 beads

Beading thread – grey (100m spool) 1

Beading needles – 1 set

Directions – String beads on thread as per diagram. When the last row is finished string through the first row to make a ring. Weave ends through 2～3 more rows and cut.

Size – Interior diameter 5.5cm/2 ¼ inches

43

Materials

Toho Beads / Mill Hill Beads

TB Beads – frosted off white (TB-762) 168 beads, frosted green (TB-940F) 77 beads, bronze (TB-221) 70 beads, orange (TB-925) 43 beads, reddish purple (TB-503) 6 beads, frosted blue (TB-43F) 14 beads, frosted purple (TB-765) 12 beads, dark pink (TB-322) 23 beads, yellow (TB-949) 7 beads

Beading thread – grey (100m spool) 1

Beading needle – (6-13-1) 1 set

Directions – Make as for ring #42.

Size – Inside diameter 5.5cm/2 ¼ inches

Diagram next page

44

Materials

Toho Beads / Mill Hill Beads

TB beads – white (TB-123) 168 beads, bronze (TB-221) 70 beads, orange (TB-925) 43 beads, yellow green (TB-457) 45 beads, gold (TB-262) 32 beads, pink (TB-906) 23 beads, frosted blue (TB-43F) and frosted purple (TB-765) 12 each, dark pink (TB-332) 8 beads, cream (TB-903) 7 beads

Beading thread – grey (100m spool) 1

Beading needle – (6-13-1) 1 set

Directions – Make as for ring #42.

Size – Inside diameter 5.5cm/2 ¼ inches

45

Materials

Toho Beads / Mill Hill Beads

TB Beads – frosted black (TB-610) 168 beads, frosted brown (TB-702) 70 beads, orange (TB-925) 43 beads, gold (TB-262) 39 beads, yellow green (TB-457) 39 beads, pink (TB-906) 23 beads, frosted blue (TB-43F) & frosted purple (TB-765) 12 beads each, red (TB-125) 8 beads, yellow (TB-949) 6 beads

Beading thread – black (100m spool) 1

Beading needles – 1 set

Directions – Make as for ring #42.

Size – Interior diameter 5.5cm/2 ¼ inches

Diagram page 65

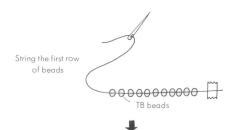

String the first row of beads

TB beads

For the second row of beads, starting on the left, string the 1st bead then thread through the 2nd bead from the 1st row.

2nd row →
1st row beads

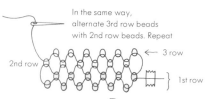

In the same way, alternate 3rd row beads with 2nd row beads. Repeat

2nd row
← 3 row
1st row

Join first and last rows as shown in diagram. Weave the ends through 2~3 rows of beads and cut

2nd row
1st row

69th row
68th row
67th row

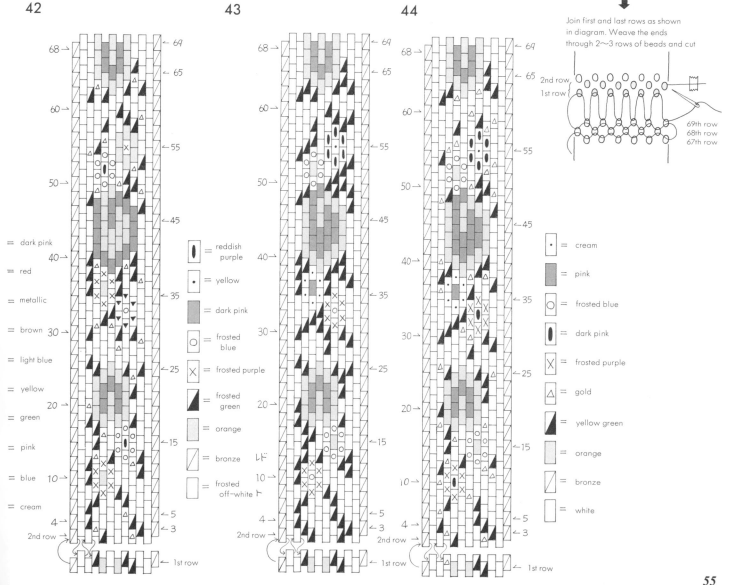

42

68 →
69
65
60 →
55
50 →
45
40 →
35
30 →
25
20 →
15
10 →
5
4 →
3
2nd row →
1st row

= dark pink
= red
= metallic
= brown
= light blue
= yellow
= green
= pink
= blue
= cream

	= reddish purple
	= yellow
	= dark pink
	= frosted blue
	= frosted purple
	= frosted green
	= orange
	= bronze
	= frosted off-white

43

68 →
69
65
60 →
55
50 →
45
40 →
35
30 →
25
20 →
15
10 →
5
3
2nd row →
1st row

44

68 →
69
65
60 →
55
50 →
45
40 →
35
30 →
25
20 →
15
10 →
5
3
2nd row →
1st row

	= cream
	= pink
	= frosted blue
	= dark pink
	= frosted purple
	= gold
	= yellow green
	= orange
	= bronze
	= white

46 PAGE 14 Ring

Materials

Toho Beads / Mill Hill Beads

Small round beads – blue (243) 80 beads, salmon pink (955) 40 beads

Bugle beads – antique gold (222) 20 beads

Nylon thread – (0.2mm diameter) 100cm/ 39 ¼ inches

Craft glue

Directions – Thread the beads on the nylon thread as shown in the diagram and form the ring. Tie the ends of the nylon thread tightly and secure with craft glue.

Size – Interior diameter 5.5cm/2 ¼ inches

47

Materials

Toho Beads / Mill Hill Beads

Small round beads – green (324) 80 beads, blue (952) 40 beads

Bugle beads (3mm) – bronze (221) 20 beads

Nylon thread – (0.2mm diameter) 100cm /39 ¼ inches

Craft glue

Directions – Make as for ring # 46.

Size – Interior diameter 5.5cm/2 ¼ inches

46·47

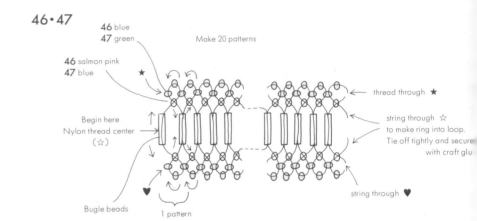

46 blue
47 green

46 salmon pink
47 blue

Make 20 patterns

★

thread through ★

string through ☆
to make ring into loop.
Tie off tightly and secure
with craft glu

Begin here
Nylon thread center
(☆)

Bugle beads

♥

string through ♥

1 pattern

48 PAGE 15 Ring

Materials

Toho Beads / Mill Hill Beads

Small round beads – amber (2) 90 beads, bronze (221) 40 beads, green (323) 30 beads, red (951) 20 beads

Nylon thread – (0.2mm diameter) 100cm/ 39 ½ inches

Craft glue

Directions – Thread the beads on the nylon thread as shown in the diagram and form the ring. Tie the ends of the nylon thread tightly and secure with craft glue.

Size – Interior diameter 5.5cm/2 ¼ inches

49

Materials

Toho Beads / Mill Hill Beads

Small round beads – cream (948) 90 beads, blue (953) 40 beads, bronze (221) 30 beads, red (951) 20 beads

Nylon thread – (0.2mm diameter) 100cm/ 39 ½ inches

Craft glue

Directions – Make as for ring #48.

Size – Interior diameter 5.5cm/2 ¼ inches

50

Materials

Toho Beads / Mill Hill Beads

Small round beads – off white (123) 90 beads, bronze (221) 40 beads, blue (952) 30 beads, orange (956) 20 beads

Nylon thread – (0.2mm diameter) 100cm/ 39 ½ inches

Craft glue

Directions – Make as for ring #48

Size – Interior diameter 5.5cm/2 ¼ inches

48·49·50

start 1st row
nylon thread center
(☆)

finish 1st row

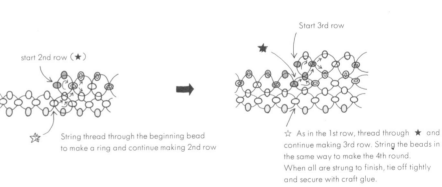

start 2nd row (★)

☆

String thread through the beginning bead
to make a ring and continue making 2nd row

Start 3rd row

★

☆ As in the 1st row, thread through ★ and
continue making 3rd row. String the beads in
the same way to make the 4th round.
When all are strung to finish, tie off tightly
and secure with craft glue.

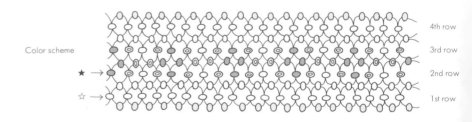

Color scheme

★ →

☆ →

4th row

3rd row

2nd row

1st row

small round beads		48	49	50
◐	=	green	bronze	blue
◔	=	red	red	orange
○	=	amber	cream	off white
◯	=	bronze	blue	bronze

51

PAGE 16
Ring

Materials

Toho Beads / Mill Hill Beads

Semi-precious maga tama beads – goldstone (a-1567) 1 bead

Beading Wire – bronze 1mm diameter – 20cm/7 ¾ inches, 0.75mm diameter – 60cm/23 ½ inches

Directions – Begin construction with 20cm of 1mm and 30cm of 0.75mm beading wire. Cut off excess later.

Size – Interior diameter 5cm/2 inches (finger circumference)

51·52·53

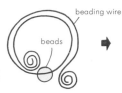  

beading wire

beads

Thread bead onto 1mm diameter wire, wrap around finger for size. Bend ends with pliers.

Wrap 0.75mm beading wire around base

On top of that wrap one more 0.75 diameter wire around

※ For illustration purposes the wire is drawn loosely, but the beading wire of the actual ring is firmly wrapped and bent.

52

Materials

Toho Beads / Mill Hill Beads

Rococo maga tama beads – white (a-1402/10mm) 1 bead

Beading wire – moss green 1mm diameter – 20cm 7¾ inches, 0.75mm diameter – 60cm/23 ¼ inches

Directions – Make as for ring #51.

Size – Interior diameter 5cm/2 inches (finger circumference)

53

Materials

Toho Beads / Mill Hill Beads

Semi-precious beads spherical – tigers eye(a-1566) 1 bead

Beading Wire – Silver 1mm diameter –20cm/ 7 ¾ inches, 0.75mm diameter – 60cm/23 ¼inches

Directions – Make as for ring #51.

Size – Interior diameter 5cm/2 inches (finger circumference)

54·55

wrap wire around velvet beads (for 54 insert the end of the wire in the hole in the bead)

velvet bead

tie off tightly twice secure with craft glue

3 cut beads

40 beads

finger circumference 5cm/2 inches (add or subtract according to finger size)

bend wire with round-nosed pliers or regular pliers

54

Materials

Toho Beads / Mill Hill Beads

Velvet Beads – black (a-1202/10mm) 1 bead

3 cut beads – bronze (CR221) 40 beads

Beading Wire – bronze (0.75mm diameter) 30cm/11 ¾ inches

Nylon thread – (0.3mm diameter) 20cm/ 7 ¾ inches

Craft glue

Directions – Wrap the velvet bead in beading wire. Press in hand so that wire grips beads. String beads on nylon thread and make ring.

Size – Interior diameter 5cm/2 inches (finger circumference)

55

Materials

Toho Beads / Mill Hill Beads

Velvet Beads – wine color (a-1205/ 10mm) 1 bead

3 cut beads – black (CR49) 40 beads

Beading wire – silver (0.75mm diameter) 30cm/11 ¾ inches

Nylon thread – (0.3mm diameter) 20cm/ 7 ¾ inches

Craft glue

Directions – Make as for ring #54.

Size – Interior diameter 5cm/2 inches (finger circumference)

56

PAGE 17
Ring

Materials

Toho Beads / Mill Hill Beads

Maga tama beads – 4mm fluorescent blue green (M307) & green (M07) 6 beads each, transparent (M21) & blue purple with transparent (M348) 5 beads each

3 cut beads – metallic (CR244) 47 beads

Nylon thread – (0.3mm diameter) 70cm

Craft glue

Directions – Make the center pattern before making round to form the ring.

Size – Interior diameter 5cm/2 inches (finger circumference)

57

Materials

Toho Beads / Mill Hill Beads

Maga tama beads – 4mm – amber (M22) & dark brown (M46) 6 beads each, brown (MO202) & transparent (M21) 5 beads each

3 cut beads – golden brown (CR421) 47 beads

Nylon thread – (0.3mm diameter) 70cm

Craft Glue

Directions – Make as for ring #56

Size – Interior diameter 5cm/2 inches (finger circumference)

56·57

start center nylon thread

3 cut beads

56 fluorescent green **57** amber

56 green **57** dark brown

56 transparent **57** brown

56 blue purple & transparent **57** transparent

maga tama beads

tie off twice tightly and secure with craft glue

2.2cm/ ¾ inch

14.5 repetitions of ♥ finger circumference 5cm/2 inches (add or subtract according to finger size)

RINGS 58 & 59 ON PAGE 65

63

PAGE 20
Earring

Materials

Toho Beads / Mill Hill Beads

Small round beads – bronze (222) 48 beads

Round pearl – dark gun metal (3mm) 32 beads, gun metal (2mm) 4 beads

Clip earring finding with clip and screw – antique bronze 1 pair

Eye pins – antique bronze (30mm) 2 pins

Nylon thread – (0.2mm diameter) 180cm/ 70 ¾ inches

Craft glue

Directions – String beads on nylon thread. When one side is done, turn over to the back and make one more side. Continue making loop. String pearl on eye pin. Put the various parts together.

Size – Refer to diagram

67

Materials

Toho Beads / Mill Hill Beads

Small round beads – bronze (222) 48 beads, metallic pink (556) 2 beads

Round pearl – gunmetal (2mm) 2 beads

Colored pearl – bronze (3mm) 32 beads

Clip Earring finding with hinge and screw – antique bronze 1 pair

Eye pin – antique bronze (30mm) 2 pins

Nylon thread – (0.2mm diameter) 180cm/ 70 ¾ inches

Craft glue

Directions – String beads on nylon thread and make as for earring #67.

Size – Refer to diagram.

64

PAGE 20
Earring

Materials

Toho Beads / Mill Hill Beads

Semi-precious beads – fancy agate (a-1541) 2 beads

Decora beads – orange (a-5605) 2 beads

Bead cap (large) – antique bronze 2 pieces

Bead cap (small) – antique bronze 2 pieces

Clip earring finding with hinge and screw – antique bronze 1 pair

Eye pin – antique bronze (30mm) 2 pins

Head pin – antique bronze (22mm) 2 pins

Directions – String beads on eye pins and head pins. Put the various parts together as per diagram.

Size – Refer to diagram

69

Materials

Toho Beads / Mill Hill Beads

Semi-precious beads – fancy agate (a-1541) 2 beads

Decora beads – beige (a-5609) 2 beads

Bead cap (large) – antique gold 2 pieces

Bead cap (small) – antique gold 2 pieces

Clip earring finding with hinge and screw – antique gold 1 pair

Eye pin – antique gold (30mm) 2 pins

Head pin – antique gold (22mm) 2 pins

Directions – Make as for earring #64.

Size – Refer to diagram.

70

Materials

Toho Beads / Mill Hill Beads

Faceted glass beads – green (a-5302/ 4mm) 2 beads

Decora beads – white (a-5603) 2 beads

Bead cap (large)– antique gold 2 pieces

Bead cap (small)– antique gold 2 pieces

Clip earring finding with hinge and screw – antique gold 1 pair

Eye pin – antique gold (30mm) 2 pins

Head pin – antique gold (22mm) 2 pins

Directions – Make as for earring #64.

Size – Refer to diagram.

63•67

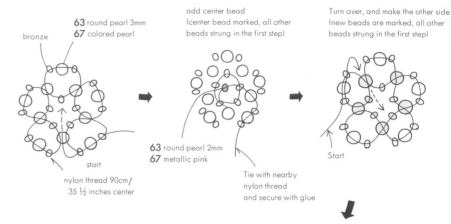

63 round pearl 3mm
67 colored pearl

bronze

add center bead (center bead marked, all other beads strung in the first step)

Turn over, and make the other side (new beads are marked, all other beads strung in the first step)

start

nylon thread 90cm/ 35 ½ inches center

63 round pearl 2mm
67 metallic pink

Start

Tie with nearby nylon thread and secure with glue

Attach pearl to the middle
Make loop on the top

bronze

tie with nearby nylon thread and secure with craft glue

63 metallic pink
67 round pearl 2mm

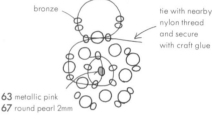

earring finding

eye pin

63 round pearl 3mm
67 colored pearl

2cm/ ¾ inch

64•69•70

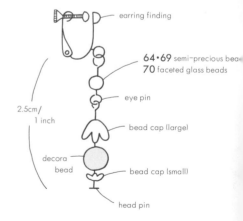

earring finding

64•69 semi-precious bead
70 faceted glass beads

eye pin

bead cap (large)

2.5cm/ 1 inch

decora bead

bead cap (small)

head pin

65 Earring

Materials

Toho Beads / Mill Hill Beads

Round pearl – gunmetal (3mm) 2 beads

Metal beads – antique silver (a-7201SF) 2 beads

Bead cap – antique silver 4 pieces

Clip earring finding with hinge and screw – antique silver 1 pair

Eye pin – antique silver (30mm) 2 pins

Head pin – antique silver (22mm) 2 pins

Jump rings – antique silver (3.8mm round) 2 pieces

Directions – String beads on eye pins and head pins. Attach various parts to make earring as in the diagram.

Size – Refer to diagram.

66

Materials

Toho Beads / Mill Hill Beads

Round pearl – enamel gold (3mm) 2 beads

Metal beads – antique gold (a-7201GF) 2 beads

Bead cap – antique gold 4 beads

Clip earring finding with hinge and screw – antique gold 1 pair

Eye pin – antique gold (30mm) 2 pins

Head pin – antique gold (22mm) 2 pins

Jump rings – antique gold (3.8mm round) 2 pieces

Directions – Make as for earring #65.

Size – Refer to diagram.

65·66

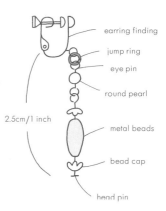

2.5cm/1 inch

earring finding
jump ring
eye pin
round pearl
metal beads
bead cap
head pin

---

68 Earring

Materials

Toho Beads / Mill Hill Beads

Small round beads – white (147) & bronze (221) 40 beads each, amber (2) & gold (557) 20 beads each

Round pearl – enameled gold (4mm) 2 beads

Crystal cut beads – topaz (J-54/4mm/#3) 2 beads

Acrylic beads – white (a-225/8mm) 2 beads

Bead cap – antique gold 4 pieces

Nylon thread – (0.2mm diameter) 60cm/23 ½ inches

Clip earring finding with hinge and screw – antique gold 1 pair

Eye pin – antique gold (30mm) 4 pins

Head pins – antique gold (22mm) 2 pins

Craft glue

Directions – String beads on nylon thread and make bead ball. String beads on eye pins and head pins. Connect parts as in diagram to make earring.

Size – Refer to diagram.

---

117 Earrings

Materials

Toho Beads / Mill Hill Beads

Small round beads – light pink (31) & bronze (222) 40 beads each, red (331) & metallic orange (551) 20 each

Colored pearls – bronze (3mm) 2 beads

Rose beads – antique gold (a-2357/ 6mm) 2 beads

Acrylic beads – orange (a-228/8mm) 2 beads

Nylon thread – (0.2mm diameter) 60cm/ 23 ½ inches

Clip earring finding with hinge and screw – antique bronze 1 pair

Eye pin – antique bronze (30mm) 4 pins

Head pin – antique bronze (22mm) 2 pins

Craft glue

Directions – Make as for earring #68.

Size – Refer to diagram.

68·117

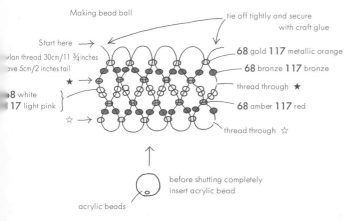

Making bead ball

Start here →

tie off tightly and secure with craft glue

nylon thread 30cm/11 ¾ inches
save 5cm/2 inches tail

68 gold 117 metallic orange

68 bronze 117 bronze

thread through ★

68 white
117 light pink

68 amber 117 red

thread through ☆

before shutting completely insert acrylic bead

acrylic beads

68

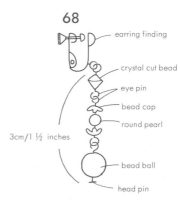

earring finding
crystal cut bead
eye pin
bead cap
round pearl

3cm/1 ½ inches

bead ball
head pin

117

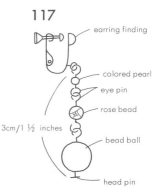

earring finding
colored pearl
eye pin
rose bead

3cm/1 ½ inches

bead ball
head pin

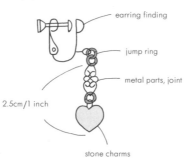
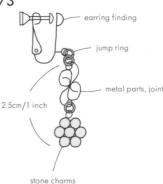

PAGE 21

71 Earring

Materials

Toho Beads / Mill Hill Beads

Stone charms – carnelian 2 pieces

Metal parts, joint – silver 2 pieces

Clip earring finding with hinge and screw – silver (9-12-8S) 1 pair

Jump ring – silver (3.8mm round) 6 pieces

Directions – Use the jump rings to fasten the pieces as shown in the diagram.

Size – Refer to the diagram.

73

Materials

Toho Beads / Mill Hill Beads

Stone charms – lavendar amethyst 2 pieces

Metal parts, joint – silver 2 pieces

Clip earring finding with hinge and screw – silver 1 pair

Jump ring – silver (3.8mm round) 6 pieces

Directions – Make as for earring #71.

Size – Refer to diagram.

72

Materials

Toho Beads / Mill Hill Beads

Decora beads – blue (a-5616) 2 beads

Maga tama beads – blue (MO3/4mm) 2 beads

Metal parts, joint – bronze 4 pieces

Clip earring finding with hinge and screw – antique gold 1 pair

Bead cap – antique silver (30mm) 2 pieces

Jump ring – antique silver (3.8 round) 6 pieces, antique gold (3.8mm round) 2 pieces

Eye pin – antique silver (30mm) 2 pins

Directions – Thread beads and bead cap on eye pin and assemble earring finding and parts with jump rings.

Size – Refer to the diagram.

72

earring finding
jump ring (antique gold)
eye pin
bead cap
decora bead
4.5cm/ 1 ¾ inches
jump ring (antique silver)
metal parts, joint
maga tama bead

71

earring finding
jump ring
metal parts, joint
2.5cm/1 inch
stone charms

73

earring finding
jump ring
metal parts, joint
2.5cm/1 inch
stone charms

PAGE 22

74 Pin

Materials

Toho Beads / Mill Hill Beads

Small round beads – black (49) 68 beads, white (147) 69 beads, cream (948) & salmon pink (955) 50 each, gold (551) 2 beads, metallic pink (556) 1 bead

3 cut beads – bronze (CR221) 218 beads

Maga tama beads – amber (M22/4mm) 1 bead

Enameled gold pearl (304) – 3mm & 4mm 1 each

Colored pearl – bronze (3mm) 1 bead

Black pearl – 3mm – 36 beads, 4mm – 2 beads

Faceted glass beads – grey (a-5309/4mm) 1 bead

Acryllic cut beads – black (a-352/6mm) 1 bead

Bead cap – antique gold 2 pieces

Eye pin – antique gold (30mm) 1 pin

Colored wire – (0.24mm diameter) silver 230cm/90 ½ inches

Pin back with rotating clasp – bronze 1

Directions – Use wire to make the separate parts and attach to ring and pin back with wire. Thread beads and bead cap on an eye pin and assemble the parts.

Size – Refer to diagram.

75

Materials

Toho Beads / Mill Hill Beads

Small round beads – metallic pink (556) 68 beads, white (147) 69 beads, grey (150) & pink (151) 50 beads each, metallic gold (557) & amber (2) 1 bead each

3 cut beads – bronze (CR222) 218 beads

Maga tama beads – amber (M22/4mm) 1 bead

Enameled gold pearl (304/3mm) 1 bead

Colored pearl – bronze (3mm) 35 beads

Faceted glass beads – grey (a-5309/4mm) 1 bead

Retro beads – antique silver (a-539/4mm) 1 bead

Crystal cut beads – amethyst (J-54-/4mm/#8) 1 bead

Semi-precious beads – lavendar amethyst (a-1544) 1 bead

Bead cap – antique bronze 2 pieces

Eye pin – antique bronze (30mm) 1 piece

Colored wire – (0.24mm diameter) silver 230cm/90 ½ inches

Pin back with rotating clasp – bronze 1

Directions – Make as for pin #75.

Size – Refer to diagram.

DIAGRAM ON NEXT PAGE.

flowers for pin base   wire 80cm/31 ½ inches make the same for both unless otherwise indicated

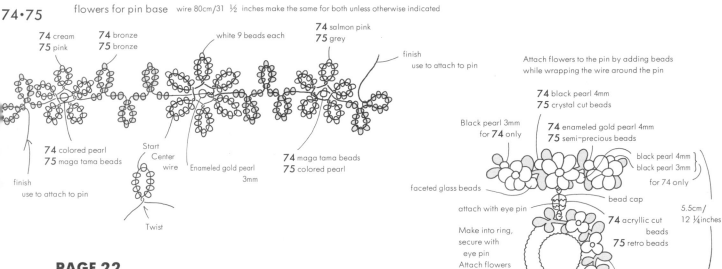

74 cream
75 pink

74 bronze
75 bronze

white 9 beads each

74 salmon pink
75 grey

finish
use to attach to pin

74 colored pearl
75 maga tama beads

Start
Center
wire

Enameled gold pearl
3mm

74 maga tama beads
75 colored pearl

finish
use to attach to pin

Twist

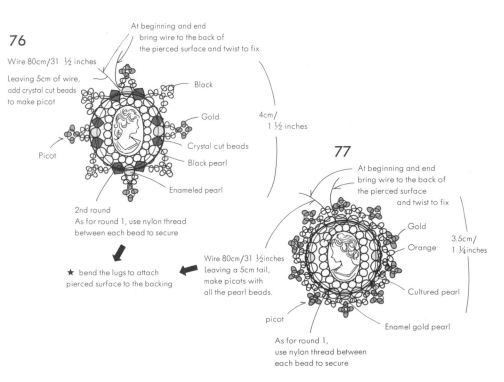

Attach flowers to the pin by adding beads
while wrapping the wire around the pin

74 black pearl 4mm
75 crystal cut beads

Black pearl 3mm
for **74** only

74 enameled gold pearl 4mm
75 semi-precious beads

black pearl 4mm
black pearl 3mm
for 74 only

faceted glass beads

bead cap

5.5cm/
12 ¼ inches

attach with eye pin

74 acryllic cut
beads
75 retro beads

Make into ring,
secure with
eye pin
Attach flowers
to ring with wire

Attach flowers to ring
with wire

Refer to **#28** on page 49 for directions
about ring construction and placement

PAGE 22

76 Pin

Materials

Toho Beads / Mill Hill Beads

Small round beads – black (49) 48 beads,
gold (557) 16 beads

Frosted gold pearl – (2.5mm) 21 beads

Black pearl – (3mm) 8 beads

Enameled gold pearl – (304/3mm) 4 beads

Crystal cut beads – black (J-54/4mm
/#10) 8 beads

Plastic cameo – red (14 × 10mm)

Nylon thread – (0.3mm diameter) 80cm/
31 ½ inches

Colored wire – (0.24mm diameter) gold
80cm/31 ½ inches

Pierced surface pin back – silver (20mm) 1

Craft glue

Directions – Fasten cameo in the center
with craft glue, secure the beads strung
in a circle twice. Make the picots around
the edges with wire.

Size – Refer to diagram.

Materials

Toho Beads / Mill Hill Beads

Small round beads – orange (924) &
gold (557) 40 each

Frosted gold pearl – (2.5mm) 21 beads

Enameled gold pearl – (304/3mm) 4 beads

Cultured pearl – (3mm) 16 pearls

Plastic cameo – red (14 × 10mm)

Nylon thread – (0.3mm diameter)
80cm/31 ½ inches

Colored wire – (0.24mm diameter) gold
80cm/31 ½ inches

Pierced surface pin back – silver (20mm) 1

Craft glue

Directions – Make as for pin #76.

Size – Refer to the diagram.

76·77

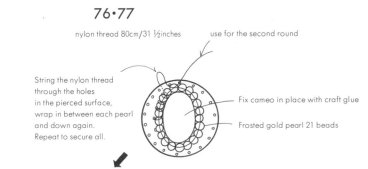

nylon thread 80cm/31 ½inches

use for the second round

String the nylon thread
through the holes
in the pierced surface,
wrap in between each pearl
and down again.
Repeat to secure all.

Fix cameo in place with craft glue

Frosted gold pearl 21 beads

76

At beginning and end
bring wire to the back of
the pierced surface and twist to fix

Wire 80cm/31 ½ inches

Leaving 5cm of wire,
add crystal cut beads
to make picot

Black

Gold

4cm/
1 ½ inches

Crystal cut beads

Black pearl

Picot

Enameled pearl

2nd round
As for round 1, use nylon thread
between each bead to secure

★ bend the lugs to attach
pierced surface to the backing

77

At beginning and end
bring wire to the back of
the pierced surface
and twist to fix

Gold

Orange

3.5cm/
1 ¼ inches

Wire 80cm/31 ½inches
leaving a 5cm tail,
make picots with
all the pearl beads.

Cultured pearl

picot

Enamel gold pearl

As for round 1,
use nylon thread between
each bead to secure

78 Pin

Materials

Toho Beads / Mill Hill Beads

Small round beads – yellow (949) 120 beads, cream (948) 125 beads, amber (103) 74 beads, light purple (110) 10 beads, bronze (222) 69 beads

TB beads – yellow green (TB-457) 286 beads, moss green (TB-940) 69 beads

Maga tama beads – amber (M22/4mm) 4 beads

Enameled gold pearl (304) 3mm & 5mm 1 each

Nylon thread – (0.2mm diameter) 20cm/ 7 ¾ inches

Colored wire – (0.35~0.37mm diameter) gold 330cm/130 inches

Pierced surface pin back – silver (24mm) 1

Ribbon – orange (4mm width) 40cm/15 ¾ inches

Directions – After assembling the various parts, secure them to the pierced surface.

Size – Refer to the diagram.

79

Materials

Toho Beads / Mill Hill Beads

Small round beads – bronze (222) 121 beads, reddish purple (115) 99 beads, purple (927) 99 beads, blue purple (926) 69 beads

TB beads – moss green (TB-940) 286 beads, frosted brown (TB-702) 69 beads, bronze (222) 10 beads

Maga tama beads – amber (M22/4mm) 4 beads

Enameled gold pearl (304) 3mm & 5mm 1 each

Nylon thread – (0.2mm diameter) 20cm/ 7 ¾ inches

Colored wire – (0.35~0.37mm diameter) gold 330cm/130 inches

Pierced surface pin back – silver (24mm) 1

Ribbon – purple (4mm width) 40cm/15 ¾ inches

Directions – Make as for pin #78.

Size – Refer to diagram.

Making the leaf
Wire 80cm/31 ½ inches

4cm/1 ½ inches

11 beads   8 beads

4cm/ 1 ½ inches

78 yellow
79 moss green

27
29
25
21
19
18
13
11
8

78 moss green
79 frosted brown

Making flower (small) Wire 40cm/15 ¾ inches

Make 4 (make 2 with 5 petals made in the same way)

Twist wire at ·
Continue making stem

Start construction

Maga tama beads

11 beads each

40 beads

cream } Make three flowers in this color scheme, 2 of them having 5 petals each
amber } Make 1 flower with the opposite color scheme

79 { reddish purple 2 (make one with 5 petals)
purple 2 (make one with 5 petals)

finish

TB beads
78 yellow green **79** moss green

finish

78·79

Make the same for both unless otherwise noted

Making flower (large)
Wire 50cm/19 ¾ inches

78 yellow
79 bronze
15 beads each

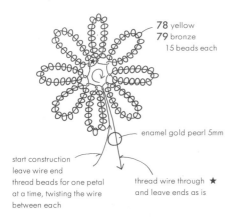

enamel gold pearl 5mm

start construction
leave wire end
thread beads for one petal
at a time, twisting the wire
between each

thread wire through ★
and leave ends as is

making flower (medium)
wire 40cm/15 ¾ inches

enamel gold pearl 3mm

start construction
leave wire as is

wrap wire at
and continue making
small flower

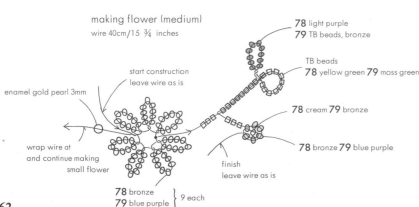

78 light purple
79 TB beads, bronze

TB beads
78 yellow green **79** moss green

78 cream **79** bronze

78 bronze **79** blue purple

finish
leave wire as is

78 bronze
79 blue purple } 9 each

thread in the following order through the holes in the pierced surface
leaf, small flower, medium flower, and large flower to the pierced surface pin
Twist the wire on the back to secure.
Secure stems with nylon thread

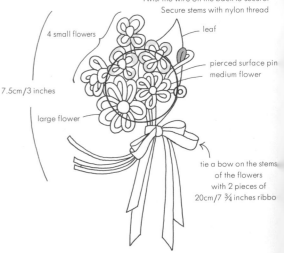

4 small flowers

leaf

pierced surface pin
medium flower

7.5cm/3 inches

large flower

tie a bow on the stems
of the flowers
with 2 pieces of
20cm/7 ¾ inches ribbon

fold down lugs on pierced surface to attach to base.

80 Pin

Materials

Toho Beads / Mill Hill Beads

Small round beads – white (123) 258 beads, bronze (221) 152 beads, brown (941) 126 beads, amber (2) 88 beads, blue purple (926) 56 beads, bronze (222) 2 beads

Maga tama beads – amber (M22/4mm) 12 beads

Enameled gold pearl (304/3mm) 1 bead

King sized beads frosted pearl – (5.5mm) 1 bead

Colored wire – (0.35～0.37mm diameter) gold 160cm/63 inches, silver 270cm/106 ¼ inches

Pierced surface pin back – silver (24mm) 1

Pin back with rotating clasp – bronze 1

Floral tape – grey

Directions – String beads on wire to make individual parts. Arrange together for balance, twist with wire, wrap with floral tape and attach to pin.

Size – Refer to diagram.

81

Materials

Toho Beads / Mill Hill Beads

Small round beads – salmon pink (955) 258 beads, bronze (222) 152 beads, metallic pink (556) 126 beads, amber (2) 88 beads, sky blue (952) 56 beads

3 cut beads – red (CR400) 2 beads

Maga tama beads – amber (M22/4mm) 12 beads

Enameled gold pearl (304/3mm) 1 bead

King sized beads – frosted yellow (22F/5.5mm) 1 bead

Colored wire – (0.35～0.37mm diameter) gold 160cm/63 inches, silver 270cm/106 ¼ inches

Pierced surface pin back – silver (24mm) 1

Pin back (swivel pin back) – bronze (9-11-11) 1

Florist's tape – grey

Directions – Make as for pin #80.

Size – Refer to diagram.

80•81   make the same for both unless otherwise indicated

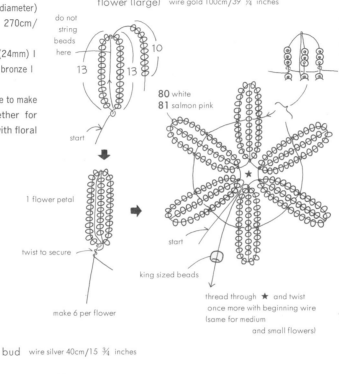

flower (large) wire gold 100cm/39 ¼ inches

do not string beads here

1 flower petal

twist to secure

make 6 per flower

80 white
81 salmon pink

king sized beads

start

thread through ★ and twist once more with beginning wire (same for medium and small flowers)

wire gold 30cm/11 ¾ inches
Wrap wire from the back between the 6th and 7th beads of each petal. (Bringing the petals together to give a three-dimensional effect.)

Leaf Wire silver 60cm/23 ½ inches
Make 2 (use opposite color scheme for 1 of them)

when finished, bring wire to the back, fold down with others and twist together

6cm/2 ¼ inches

4cm/1 ½ inches

80 brown
81 metallic pink

80 bronze
81 bronze

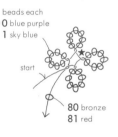

flower (small) wire silver 30cm/11 ¾ inches
make 2

beads each
0 blue purple
1 sky blue

start

80 bronze
81 red

head of grain wire gold 30cm

start

maga tama beads

thread maga tama beads in numerical order on wire and twist

bud wire silver 40cm/15 ¾ inches

start

80 white
81 salmon pink

80 brown
81 metallic pink

80 bronze
81 bronze

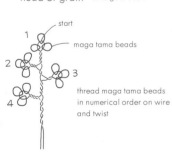

flower (medium)
wire silver 50cm/19 ¾ inches

amber 11 beads each

start

enamel gold pearl

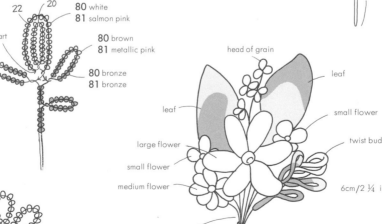

head of grain

leaf

leaf

large flower

small flower

medium flower

small flower

twist bud

arrange for overall balance twist the wire wrap with florist tape

fold up

back

6cm/2 ¼ inches

use 20cm silver wire to wrap the pin back on to secure ☆

82 Pin

Materials

Toho Beads / Mill Hill Beads

Small round beads – blue (953) 148 beads, cream (949) 114 beads, amber (2) 90 beads, white (123) 49 beads

3 cut beads – red (CR400) 203 beads

Colored wire – (0.24mm diameter) silver 365cm/143 ¾ inches

Pierced surface pin back – silver (14mm) 1

Directions – Assemble individual parts before securing to pierced surface.

Size – Refer to diagram.

83

Materials

Toho Beads / Mill Hill Beads

Small round beads – light orange (955) 180 beads, green (324) 148 beads, orange (956) 131 beads, blue (143) 90 beads, white (123) 49 beads, bronze (222) 6 beads

Colored wire – (0.24mm diameter) silver 325cm/128 inches

Pierced surface pin back – silver (14mm) 1

Directions – Make as for pin #82.

Size – Refer to diagram.

Making the rose (large)

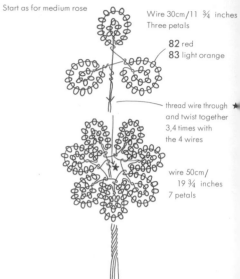

Start as for medium rose

Wire 30cm/11 ¾ inches
Three petals

82 red
83 light orange

thread wire through ★ and twist together 3,4 times with the 4 wires

wire 50cm/ 19 ¾ inches 7 petals

82·83

making the rose (medium)
wire 40cm/15 ¾ inches

thread the inner beads and twist before threading outer beads and wrapping

outer 13 beads
inner 5 beads

wrap at (continue making the required number of petals)

start

finish
twist with beginning end 3.4 times

82 cream
83 orange

6 petals

start

10cm

making small flower   wire 15cm/6 inches

make 3

82 amber
83 blue

82 cream
83 bronze

thread through ★

start

making leaf
wire 40cm/15 ¾ inches

make 2

start

the same as for Leaf on page 63

9

11

3

6

82 blue 83 green

making mini rose   wire 20cm/7 ¾ inches

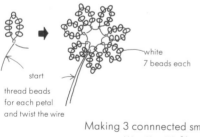

white
7 beads each

start

thread beads for each petal and twist the wire

thread through the pierced surface, wrap on the back to secure in the following order: leaf, large rose, medium rose, mini rose, bud, 3 connected small flowers, small flower.

medium rose

3 connected small flowers

leaf

leaf

pierced surface pin back

mini rose

large rose

4.5cm/ 1 ¾ inches

small flower

bud

82 blue
83 green

to cover gaps thread 12 beads each as shown in the diagram and add to 4 places

wire 20cm

Secure the lugs to attach pierced surface to the backing

Making 3 connnected small flowers
Wire 50cm/19 ¾ inches

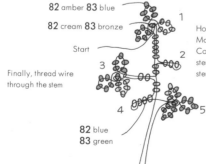

82 amber 83 blue

82 cream 83 bronze

Start

1

2

3

4

5

Finally, thread wire through the stem

82 blue
83 green

How to make small flower
Make flower #1.
Continue making, stem, leaf, stem, flower #3, stem, leaf #4 and flower #5

Making the bud
wire 30cm/11 ¾ inches

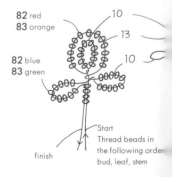

82 red
83 orange

82 blue
83 green

10

13

10

finish

Start
Thread beads in the following order: bud, leaf, stem

84 PAGE 24 Bracelet

Materials

Toho Beads / Mill Hill Beads

3 cut beads – bronze (CR-221) 82 beads

Accessory cord (with 4 crimp beads) – silver 240cm/94 ½ inches

Clasp set – bronze 1 set

Directions – Cut accessory cord into 4 pieces 60cm/23 ½ inches each. Use in pairs as shown in diagram.

Size – Refer to diagram.

85

Materials

Toho Beads / Mill Hill Beads

3 cut beads – black (CR-49) 82 beads

Accessory cord (with 4 crimp beads) – silver 240cm/94 ½ inches

Clasp set – bronze 1 set

Directions – Make as for bracelet #84.

Size – Refer to Diagram.

84·85

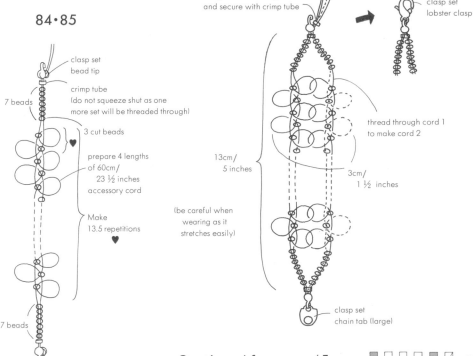

bring the 4 cords together and secure with crimp tube

clasp set lobster clasp

clasp set bead tip

crimp tube (do not squeeze shut as one more set will be threaded through)

7 beads

3 cut beads

prepare 4 lengths of 60cm/ 23 ½ inches accessory cord

Make 13.5 repetitions ♥

thread through cord 1 to make cord 2

13cm/ 5 inches

3cm/ 1 ½ inches

(be careful when wearing as it stretches easily)

7 beads

clasp set chain tab (large)

58 PAGE 17 Ring

Materials

Toho Beads / Mill Hill Beads

Maga tama beads – 4mm brown (MO202) & dark brown (M46) 6 beads each, red (M45) red & red with transparent (MO105) 4 beads each

3 cut beads – bronze (CR221) 62 beads

Nylon thread – (0.3mm diameter) 50cm/ 19 ¾ inches

Craft glue

Directions – Start in the center of the nylon thread. To leave no spaces between the maga tama beads, alternate the direction of the beads.

Size – Interior diameter 5cm/2 inches (finger circumference)

59

Materials

Toho Beads / Mill Hill Beads

Maga tama beads – 4mm light blue (M23) & blue purple with transparent (M348) 6 beads each, blue (M48) & indigo (MO8) 4 beads each

3 cut beads – bronze (CR221) 62 beads

Nylon thread – (0.3mm diameter) 50cm/ 19 ¾ inches

Craft glue

Directions – Make as for ring #58.

Size – Interior diameter 5cm/2 inches (finger circumference)

58·59

cross at the mark (★) and thread through. Tie off tightly twice and secure with craft glue

58 brown 59 light blue

58 red and transparent 59 blue

58 dark brown 59 blue purple and transparent

58 red 59 indigo

maga tama beads

1.2cm/ ½inch

start center of nylon thread

make 19.5 repetitions of ♥ finger circumference 5cm/2 inches (add or subtract to adjust to finger size)

3 cut beads

Continued from page 55

45

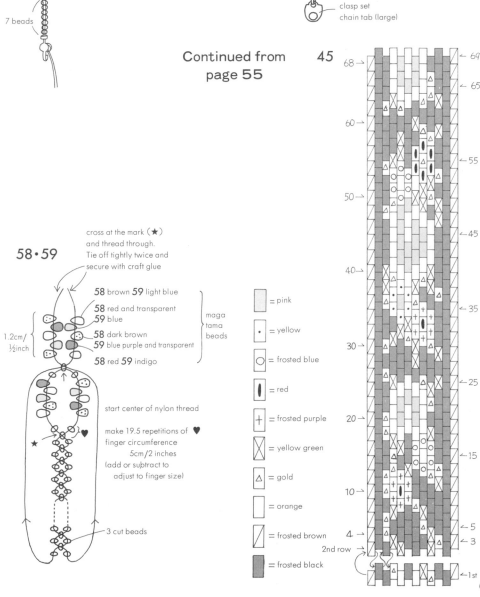

68 →

60 →

50 →

40 →

30 →

10 →

4 →

2nd row

1st row

← 69

← 65

← 55

← 45

← 35

← 25

← 15

← 5

← 3

= pink

= yellow

= frosted blue

= red

= frosted purple

= yellow green

= gold

= orange

= frosted brown

= frosted black

95 Barrette

Materials

Toho Beads / Mill Hill Beads

Metal beads – antique silver (a–7203 SF) 1 bead

Barrette with acrylic base – black 1

Ribbon – gold lame (24mm width) 18cm/ 7 inches, silver lame (24mm width) 10cm/ 4 inches

Craft glue

Directions – Attach silver lame ribbon to barrette base. Make a flower with the gold lame ribbon and attach to barrette.

Size – Refer to diagram.

96

Materials

Toho Beads / Mill Hill Beads

Maga tama beads – amber (M22/4mm) 21 beads

Barrette back – gold (56mm) 1

Ribbon – orange to green gradation (25mm width) 30cm/11 ¾ inches

Directions – Make a running stitch through the ribbon and gather. Attach barrette to the back. Sew beads in the middle.

Size – Refer to diagram.

97

Materials

Barrette with acrylic base – black 1

Ribbon – gold lame (24mm width) 10cm, orange (25mm width) & brown with blue (25mm width) & green (25mm width) 15cm/ 6 inches each

Craft glue

Directions – Attach gold lame ribbon to the barrette base Make a flower with the other ribbon and attach to the barrette.

Size – Refer to diagram.

97

make flower

ribbon { (4563) 2 kinds / (4650)

running stitch through middle

shape the gathered ribbon into a flower

the same as barrette #95, attach ribbon (3088) on top of barrette

place the 3 flowers in a row and stitch on

barrette with acrylic base

7cm/ 2 ¾ inches

95

acrylic base barrette (back view)

1cm/ ½ inch

1cm/ ½ inch

gold lame ribbon

fold ends of ribbon, sew in place and secure with craft glue

metal beads

make the gold lame ribbon the same as for ② of hair band #98

sew in place

barrette (front view)

7cm/ 2 ¾ inches

96

make as for barrette #99

① Sew a running stitch though 7cm/2 ¾ inches of ribbon and gather.

② Sew the barrette to the back. Fold the ends of the ribbon and sew in place

③ Sew beads in place

6.5cm/ 2 ½ inches

98 Hair band

Materials

Toho Beads / Mill Hill Beads

3 cut beads – brown (CR421) 39 beads

Maga tama beads 4mm – brown (MO202) 7 beads, amber (M22) 5 beads

Metal beads – antique gold (a–7203GF) 1 bead

Ribbon – mustard (50mm width) 45cm, black and gold lame (24mm width) 18cm/ 7 inches

Store bought fabric covered hair band kit – 1

Craft glue

Directions – Cut the mustard colored ribbon to the size of the hair band and glue in place to make the base. Make a flower with the lame ribbon. Sew the flower and beads to the base.

Size – 2.5cm/1 inch width

Diagram next page

① Make base

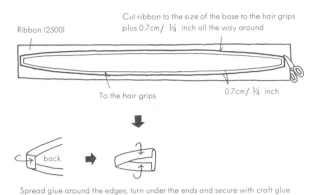

Ribbon (2500)

Cut ribbon to the size of the base to the hair grips plus 0.7cm/ ¼ inch all the way around

To the hair grips

0.7cm/ ¼ inch

back

Spread glue around the edges, turn under the ends and secure with craft glue

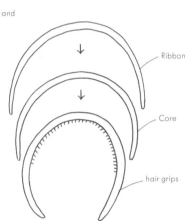

Use only core and hair grips of store bought hair band

Affix ribbon, core and hair grips with craft glue

Ribbon

Core

hair grips

② make flower

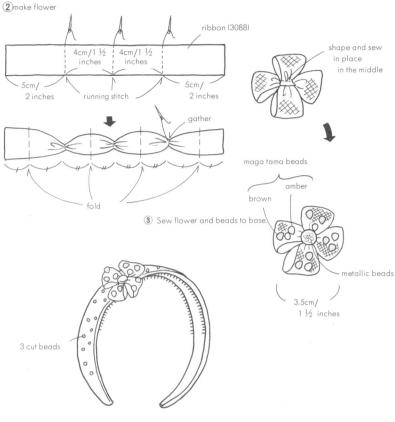

ribbon (3088)

4cm/1 ½ inches

4cm/1 ½ inches

5cm/ 2 inches

running stitch

5cm/ 2 inches

gather

fold

shape and sew in place in the middle

③ Sew flower and beads to base

maga tama beads

brown

amber

metallic beads

3.5cm/ 1 ½ inches

3 cut beads

ribbon

(2500)   (4563)

with 2 ribbons together, sew a running stitch

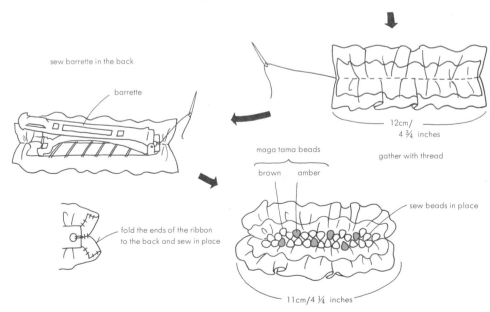

12cm/ 4 ¾ inches

gather with thread

sew barrette in the back

barrette

fold the ends of the ribbon to the back and sew in place

maga tama beads

brown   amber

sew beads in place

11cm/4 ¼ inches

99 PAGE 29 Barrette

Materials

Toho Beads / Mill Hill Beads

Maga tama beads – 4mm brown (MO202) 24 beads, amber (M22) 6 beads

Barrette back – gold (85mm) I

Ribbon – green (50mm width) 23cm/9 inches, purple (25mm width) 23cm /9 inches

Directions – With 2 ribbons together, sew a running stitch, gather, attach barrette to the back. Sew beads in the center.

Size – Refer to diagram.

102 Mini bag

102

Materials

Toho Beads / Mill Hill Beads

3 cut beads – clear aurora (CR141) 591 beads

Twisted bugle beads – clear aurora (161/12mm) 240 beads

Jump ring – silver (5mm round) 4 pieces

Purse frame – silver (9.5cm width) 1

Beading thread – white (100m spool) 1

Nylon thread – (0.3mm diameter) 90cm/35½ inches

Ribbon – grey (100mm width) 20cm/7¾ inches

Craft glue

Directions – Make the ribbon into a bag, attach to the purse frame, attach beads to bag. String beads on nylon thread to make strap and attach to purse frame with jump rings.

Size – bag 10cm × 8cm/4 × 3¼inches, strap approximately 70cm/27½inches long

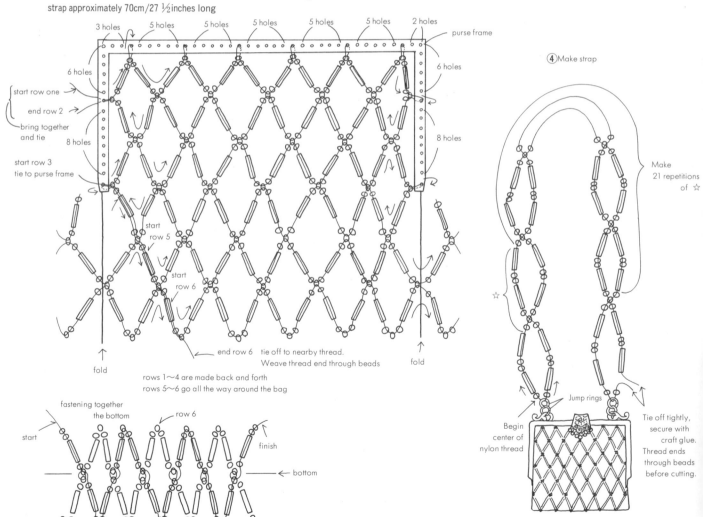

① make the bag

fold ribbon and sew up the sides

fold 2cm/¾ inches

8cm/3¼ inches

Ribbon

fold

10cm/4 inches

ship stitch 3.5cm/1¼ inches

② Sew to the purse frame

purse frame

fold under both sides to fit the purse frame

Bag

③ Attach beads

Bag (lining)

start row 1

6 holes

5 holes

5 holes

3 holes

2 holes

Push needle to the front side at the edge of the purse frame

twisted bugle beads

3 cut beads

3 holes   5 holes   5 holes   5 holes   5 holes   5 holes   2 holes   purse frame

6 holes

start row one

end row 2

bring together and tie

8 holes

start row 3
tie to purse frame

6 holes

8 holes

④ Make strap

Make 21 repetitions of ☆

☆

start row 5

start row 6

fold

end row 6   tie off to nearby thread.
Weave thread end through beads

fold

rows 1~4 are made back and forth
rows 5~6 go all the way around the bag

fastening together the bottom

start

row 6

row 6

finish

bottom

Jump rings

Begin center of nylon thread

Tie off tightly, secure with craft glue. Thread ends through beads before cutting.

03 Bag

Materials

Toho Beads / Mill Hill Beads

King sized beads – frosted bronze (702) 4mm – 134 beads, 5.5mm – 76 beads

TB beads – brownish green (TB262) 16 beads

Decora beads – antique gold (a–5609) 4 beads

Accent ball – gold (6mm) 8 beads

Bead cap – antique gold 4 pieces

Eye pin – antique gold (30mm) 50 pins

Purse frame – gold (6cm width) 1

Ribbon – orange (25mm width tubular), grey (25mm width tubular) 60cm/23½ inches each, ultra marine (25mm width), light pink ×blue (25mm width), purple (25mm width), blue (25mm width) and greenish (25mm width) 30cm/11 ¾ inches each

Directions – Weave ribbon as shown in diagram, make bag, attach to purse frame. String beads on eye pins, assemble strap and attach to bag. Sew beads to bottom of bag.

Size – bag 10cm × 12.5cm/4 × 5 inches, strap 94cm/37 inches long

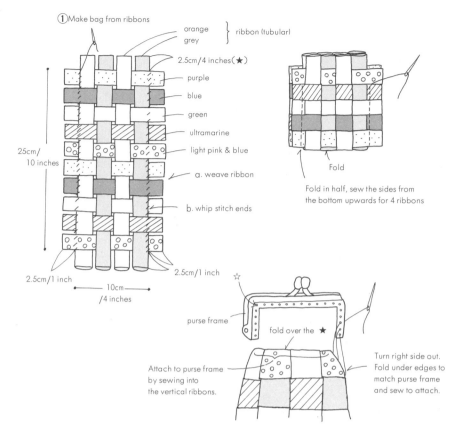

① Make bag from ribbons

orange
grey } ribbon (tubular)

2.5cm/4 inches (★)

purple
blue
green
ultramarine
light pink & blue

a. weave ribbon

b. whip stitch ends

25cm/10 inches

2.5cm/1 inch

10cm/4 inches

2.5cm/1 inch

Fold

Fold in half, sew the sides from the bottom upwards for 4 ribbons

purse frame

fold over the ★

Attach to purse frame by sewing into the vertical ribbons.

Turn right side out. Fold under edges to match purse frame and sew to attach.

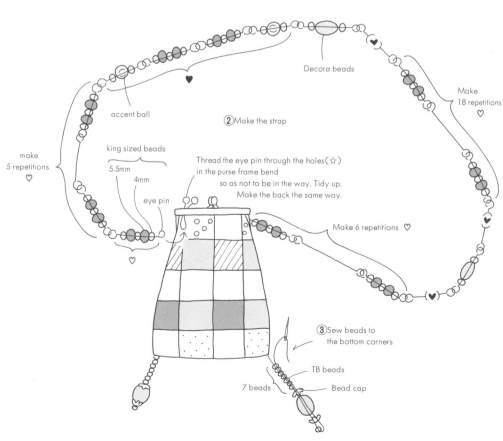

Decora beads

Make 18 repetitions ♡

accent ball

② Make the strap

Make 6 repetitions ♡

make 5 repetitions ♡

king sized beads

5.5mm

4mm

eye pin

Thread the eye pin through the holes (☆) in the purse frame bend so as not to be in the way. Tidy up. Make the back the same way.

③ Sew beads to the bottom corners

TB beads

7 beads

Bead cap

104 PAGE 32 Pouch

Materials

Toho Beads / Mill Hill Beads

Small round beads – amber (2) 3232 beads, transparent gold (103) 2888 beads, gold (557) 162 beads, bronze (221) 20 beads

King sized beads gold – (22F) 84 beads

Frosted gold pearl – (3mm) 96 beads, (6 mm) 42 beads, (oval 3 × 6mm) 36 beads

Round pearl – enameled gold (10mm) 2 beads

Crystal cut beads – topaz (J-54/4mm/ #3) 4 beads

Nylon thread – (0.3mm diameter) 900cm/ 354 ¼ inches

Lining fabric – 43cm × 19cm/17 × 7 ½ inches

Craft glue

Directions – String beads on nylon thread and make the bottom. Using other thread, make sides. Make drawstrings and thread them through the loops. Make the lining and attach.

Size – Refer to diagram.

105

Materials

Toho Beads / Mill Hill Beads

Small round beads – grey (113) 3400 beads, purple (110) 2880 beads, gun metal (81) 22 beads

Square beads – purple (69/3mm) 84 beads

Round pearl – gun metal 4mm – 96 beads, 6mm – 42 beads

Oval pearl – gun metal (3 × 6mm) 72 beads

Acrylic beads – pink (a-203/10mm) 2 beads

Crystal cut beads – amethyst (J-54/ 4mm/#8) 4 beads

Nylon thread – (0.3mm diameter) 900cm/ 354 ¼ inches

Lining fabric – 43cm × 19cm/17 × 7 ½ inches

Craft glue

Directions – Make as for pouch #104.

Size – Refer to diagram.

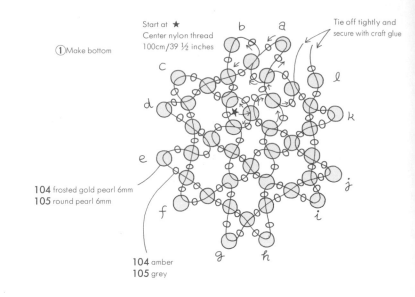

① Make bottom

Start at ★
Center nylon thread
100cm/39 ½ inches

Tie off tightly and secure with craft glue

b a c d e f g h i j k l

104 frosted gold pearl 6mm
105 round pearl 6mm

104 amber
105 grey

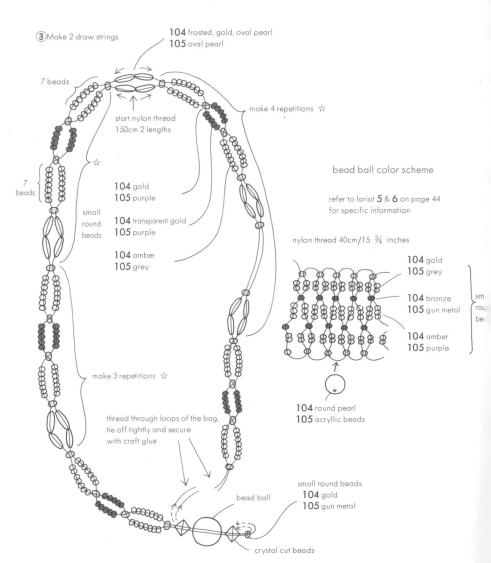

③ Make 2 draw strings

104 frosted, gold, oval pearl
105 oval pearl

7 beads

start nylon thread
150cm 2 lengths

make 4 repetitions ☆

7 beads

small round beads

104 gold
105 purple

104 transparent gold
105 purple

104 amber
105 grey

make 3 repetitions ☆

thread through loops of the bag, tie off tightly and secure with craft glue

bead ball

small round beads
104 gold
105 gun metal

crystal cut beads

bead ball color scheme

refer to lariat **5** & **6** on page 44 for specific information

nylon thread 40cm/15 ¾ inches

104 gold
105 grey

104 bronze
105 gun metal

sm rou be

104 amber
105 purple

104 round pearl
105 acryllic beads

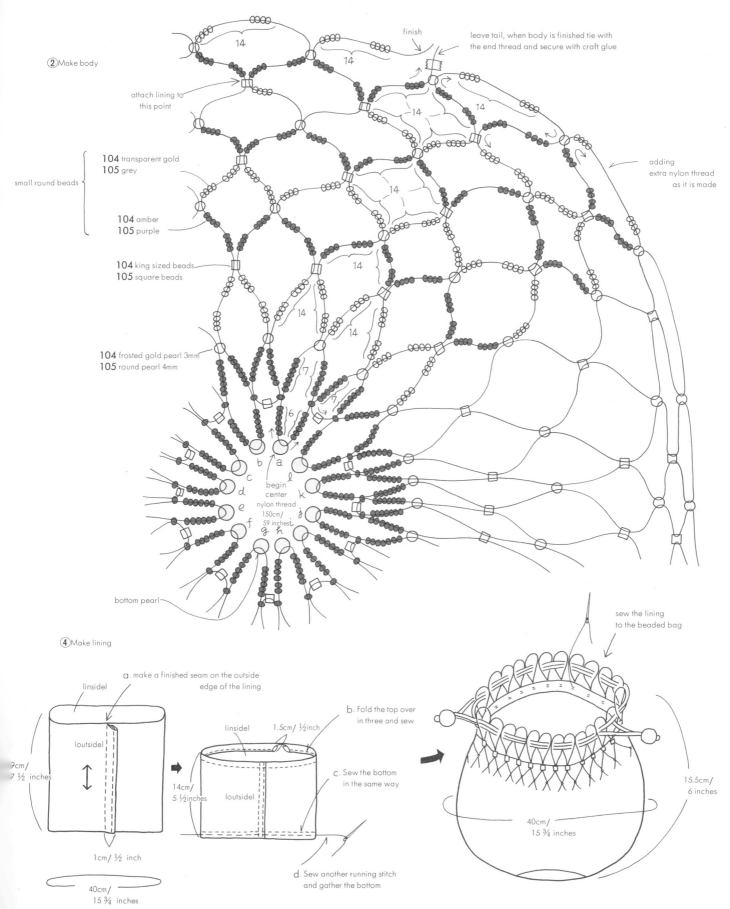

② Make body

finish

leave tail, when body is finished tie with
the end thread and secure with craft glue

14

14

14

14

attach lining to
this point

adding
extra nylon thread
as it is made

small round beads

104 transparent gold
105 grey

104 amber
105 purple

104 king sized beads
105 square beads

14

14

14

14

104 frosted gold pearl 3mm
105 round pearl 4mm

7

7

6

b a
c
d l
e k
f j
g h

begin
center
nylon thread
150cm/
59 inches

bottom pearl

④ Make lining

sew the lining
to the beaded bag

a. make a finished seam on the outside
edge of the lining

(inside)

(inside)

b. Fold the top over
in three and sew

1.5cm/ ½inch

(outside)

(outside)

c. Sew the bottom
in the same way

9cm/
7 ½ inches

14cm/
5 ½inches

15.5cm/
6 inches

1cm/ ½ inch

d. Sew another running stitch
and gather the bottom

40cm/
15 ¾ inches

40cm/
15 ¾ inches

71

106 Bag

Materials

Toho Beads / Mill Hill Beads

Small round beads – bronze (222) 330 beads, blue (953) 166 beads

Royal beads (small round) frosted purple (704) 10 beads

Royal bugle beads – pinkish (703/6mm) 69 beads

Acrylic beads – purple (a-205/10mm) 1 bead

Nylon thread – (0.2mm diameter) 290cm /114 ¼ inches

Shantung – metallic 30cm × 36cm/113/4 ×14 ¼ inches

Lining fabric – 30cm × 36cm/113/4 ×14 ¾ inches

Heavy weight interfacing – 32cm × 47cm/121/2 × 18 ½ inches

Craft glue

Directions – String beads on nylon thread. Cut out the fabric and make bag. Arrange the beaded motif on the bag for balance and sew to attach.

Size – Refer to diagram.

107

Materials

Toho Beads / Mill Hill Beads

Small round beads – bronze (222) 420 beads, purple (926) 112 beads, blue (929) 232 beads

Twisted bugle beads – brown (702/9mm) 141 beads

Royal bugle beads – grey (612/6mm) 57 beads

Crimp beads – 2 beads

Nylon thread – (0.2mm diameter) 250cm/ 98 ½ inches, (0.3mm diameter) 400cm/ 157 ½ inches

Ribbon – brown (10mm width) 10cm/4 inches

Shantung – Brown 21.5cm × 32cm/81/ 2 × 12 ½ inches

Lining – 32cm × 21.5cm/121/2 × 8 ½ inches

Heavy weight interfacing – 43cm × 32cm/17 × 13 inches

Craft Glue

Directions – Thread the beads on nylon thread (0.3mm diameter) to make shoulder strap starting at the ribbon loops. The remaining directions are the same as for #106.

Size – Refer to diagram.

Making the Motif
Nylon thread 250cm/98 ½ inches

106 make 8 repetitions of ♥
107 make 6 repetitions of ♥

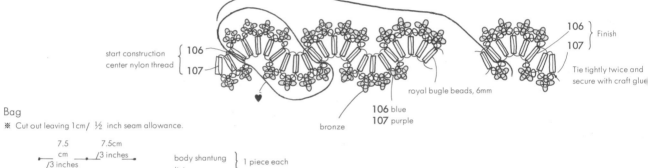

start construction
center nylon thread
106
107

106
107 } Finish

Tie tightly twice and secure with craft glue

royal bugle beads, 6mm

106 blue
107 purple

bronze

Bag
※ Cut out leaving 1cm/ ½ inch seam allowance.

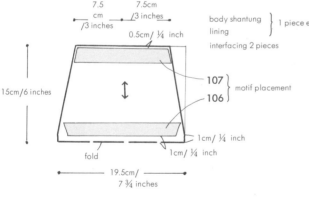

7.5 cm /3 inches   7.5cm /3 inches

0.5cm/ ¼ inch

body shantung
lining   } 1 piece each
interfacing 2 pieces

107
106 } motif placement

15cm/6 inches

1cm/ ¼ inch
1cm/ ¼ inch

fold

19.5cm/ 7 ¾ inches

106 handle · loop
※ Cut out

shantung
interfacing } 1 each

4cm/ 1 ½ inches

handle

30cm/ 11 ¾ inches

106 loop

2cm/ ¾ inch

1 piece shantung

8cm /3 ¼ inches

106

making the bead ball
nylon thread 40cm/15 ¾ inches

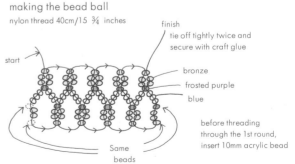

finish
tie off tightly twice and secure with craft glue

start

bronze
frosted purple
blue

before threading through the 1st round, insert 10mm acrylic bead

Same beads

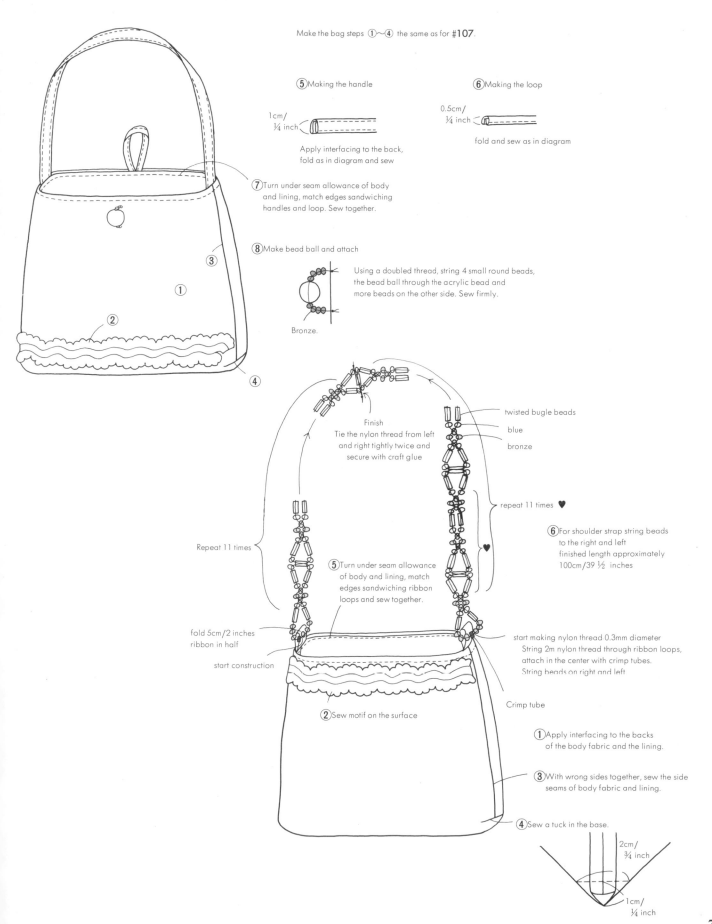

Make the bag steps ①~④ the same as for #107.

⑤ Making the handle

1cm/ ¼ inch

Apply interfacing to the back, fold as in diagram and sew

⑥ Making the loop

0.5cm/ ¼ inch

fold and sew as in diagram

⑦ Turn under seam allowance of body and lining, match edges sandwiching handles and loop. Sew together.

⑧ Make bead ball and attach

Using a doubled thread, string 4 small round beads, the bead ball through the acrylic bead and more beads on the other side. Sew firmly.

Bronze.

③

①

②

④

twisted bugle beads

blue

bronze

Finish
Tie the nylon thread from left and right tightly twice and secure with craft glue

repeat 11 times ♥

Repeat 11 times

⑥ For shoulder strap string beads to the right and left finished length approximately 100cm/39 ½ inches

⑤ Turn under seam allowance of body and lining, match edges sandwiching ribbon loops and sew together.

♥

fold 5cm/2 inches ribbon in half

start construction

start making nylon thread 0.3mm diameter
String 2m nylon thread through ribbon loops, attach in the center with crimp tubes.
String beads on right and left

② Sew motif on the surface

Crimp tube

① Apply interfacing to the backs of the body fabric and the lining.

③ With wrong sides together, sew the side seams of body fabric and lining.

④ Sew a tuck in the base.

2cm/ ¾ inch

1cm/ ¼ inch

108 PAGE 34 Pouch

Materials

Toho Beads / Mill Hill Beads

Small round beads – black (49) 504 beads

Beading thread – black (100m spool) I

Velveteen – pink 44cm × 20.5cm/171/ 4 × 8inches

Lining fabric – 44cm × 16.5cm/171/4 × 6 ½ inches

Cording ribbon – Black (3mm diameter) 120cm/47 ¼ inches

Directions – As shown in the diagram, make the bag, sew on the beads and insert drawstring.

Size – Refer to diagram.

109

Materials

Toho Beads / Mill Hill Beads

Small round beads – brown (941) 336 beads, bronze (221) 168 beads

Beading thread – beige (100m spool) I

Velveteen – beige 44cm × 20.5cm/171/ 4 × 8 inches

Lining fabric – 44cm × 16.5cm/171/4 × 6 ½ inches

Cording ribbon – brown (3mm diameter) 120cm/147 ¼ inches

Directions – Make as for pouch #108.

Size – Refer to diagram.

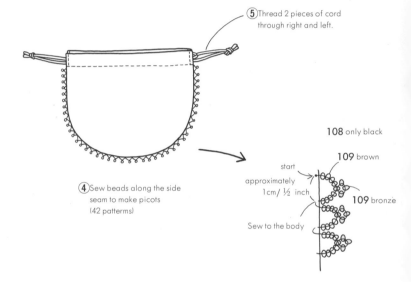

※ Cut out fabric adding seam allowances indicated in ( ).

velveteen lining } 2 pieces each

velveteen (3) lining (1)

2cm/ ¾ inch

2cm/ ¾ inch

slit in the velveteen

velveteen 16.5cm/ 6 ½inches
lining 14.5cm/ 5 ¾inches

(1)cm/ ½ inch (1cm/ ½ inch)

8cm

3.5cm 1 ¼ inch

8cm /3 ¼inches

20cm/ 7 ¾ inches

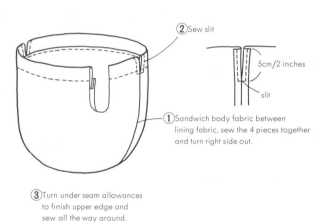

② Sew slit

5cm/2 inches

slit

① Sandwich body fabric between lining fabric, sew the 4 pieces together and turn right side out.

③ Turn under seam allowances to finish upper edge and sew all the way around.

⑤ Thread 2 pieces of cord through right and left.

④ Sew beads along the side seam to make picots (42 patterms)

108 only black

109 brown

start approximately 1cm/ ½ inch

109 bronze

Sew to the body

110 PAGE 34 Amulet bag

Materials

Toho Beads / Mill Hill Beads

Small round beads – greenish (323) 1042 beads

Twisted bugle beads – frosted brown (702/12mm) 148 beads

Nylon thread – (0.3mm diameter) 680cm/ 367 ¾ inches

Craft glue

Directions – String beads on nylon thread to make the body of the bag. Close bottom. String beads on an additional piece of nylon thread to make strap.

Size – Refer to diagram.

111

Materials

Toho Beads / Mill Hill Beads

Small round beads – bronze (222) 452 beads

Royal beads, small round – frosted deep red (703) 590 beads

Twisted bugle beads – bronze (221/12mm) 148 beads

Nylon thread – (0.3mm diameter) 680 beads

Craft glue

Directions – Make as for amulet bag #110.

Size – Refer to diagram.

DIAGRAM ON NEXT PAGE

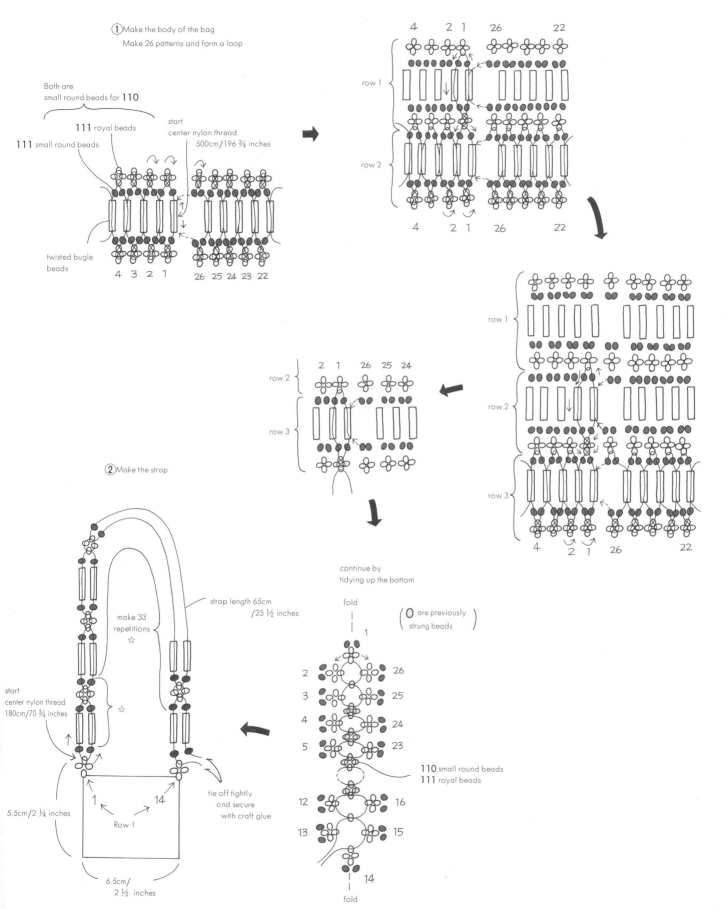

① Make the body of the bag
Make 26 patterns and form a loop

Both are
small round beads for **110**

111 royal beads

111 small round beads

start
center nylon thread
500cm/196 ¾ inches

twisted bugle
beads

4 3 2 1   26 25 24 23 22

4   2 1   26   22

row 1

row 2

4   2 1   26   22

row 1

row 2

row 3

4   2 1   26   22

2 1   26 25 24

row 2

row 3

② Make the strap

make 33
repetitions
☆

strap length 65cm
/25 ½ inches

start
center nylon thread
180cm/70 ¾ inches

☆

5.5cm/2 ¼ inches

1   14

Row 1

tie off tightly
and secure
with craft glue

6.5cm/
2 ½ inches

continue by
tidying up the bottom

fold

1

(**0** are previously
strung beads)

2   26

3   25

4   24

5   23

110 small round beads
111 royal beads

12   16

13   15

14

fold

112 Bag

112

Materials

Toho Beads / Mill Hill Beads

Acryllic beads – grey (a-226/12mm) 12 beads

Maga tama beads – transparent (M21/4mm) 10 beads

3 cut beads – grey (CR112) 120 beads

Eye pin – antique silver (30mm) 12 pins

Jump ring – bronze (5mm round) 13 pieces

Purse frame – silver (11.5cm/4 ½ inches width)

Beading thread – grey (100m spool) 1

Velveteen – dark grey 20cm × 36cm/7 ¾ × 14 ¼ inches

Directions – Make bag as in diagram, Sew on the beads. Make handle.

Size – Refer to diagram.

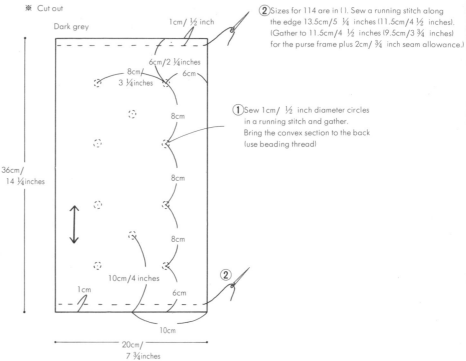

※ Cut out

Dark grey

1cm/ ½ inch

6cm/2 ¼ inches
8cm/
3 ¼ inches
6cm
8cm
8cm
8cm
8cm
10cm/4 inches
1cm
6cm
10cm

36cm/
14 ¼ inches

20cm/
7 ¾ inches

② Sizes for 114 are in ( ). Sew a running stitch along the edge 13.5cm/5 ¼ inches (11.5cm/4 ½ inches). (Gather to 11.5cm/4 ½ inches (9.5cm/3 ¾ inches) for the purse frame plus 2cm/ ¾ inch seam allowance.)

① Sew 1cm/ ½ inch diameter circles in a running stitch and gather. Bring the convex section to the back (use beading thread)

②

③ Fold from top 1.5cm/ ½ inch, 1cm/ ½ inch each side. Sew 2~3mm inside the fold line to match the holes of the purse frame

2~3mm

1.5cm/ ½ inch

② Running stitch position (back side)

1cm/ ½ inch

purse frame

1.5cm/ ½ inch

purse frame (back)

③

④ Reinforce again with overhand stitches.

Lining

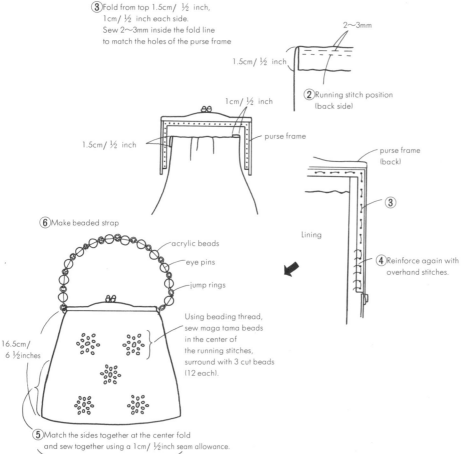

⑥ Make beaded strap

acrylic beads

eye pins

jump rings

16.5cm/
6 ½inches

Using beading thread, sew maga tama beads in the center of the running stitches, surround with 3 cut beads (12 each).

⑤ Match the sides together at the center fold and sew together using a 1cm/ ½inch seam allowance.

18cm/
7 inches

113

Materials

Toho Beads / Mill Hill Beads

Royal twisted bugle beads – 12mm metallic (512) 45 beads, aurora (86) 30 beads

Maga tama beads – transparent (M21/4mm) 93 beads

3 cut beads – aurora (CR86) 98 beads

Royal twisted bugle beads, 3 cut – silver (CR713) 40 beads

Jump ring – silver (5mm round) 8 pieces

Purse frame – silver (12.5cm/5 inches width) 1

Beading thread – grey (100m spool) 1

Nylon thread – #6 40cm/15 ¾ inches

Shantung – blue purple 21cm × 35cm/8 ¼ × 13 ¾ inches

Craft glue

Directions – Make as for bag #112.

Size – Refer to diagram.

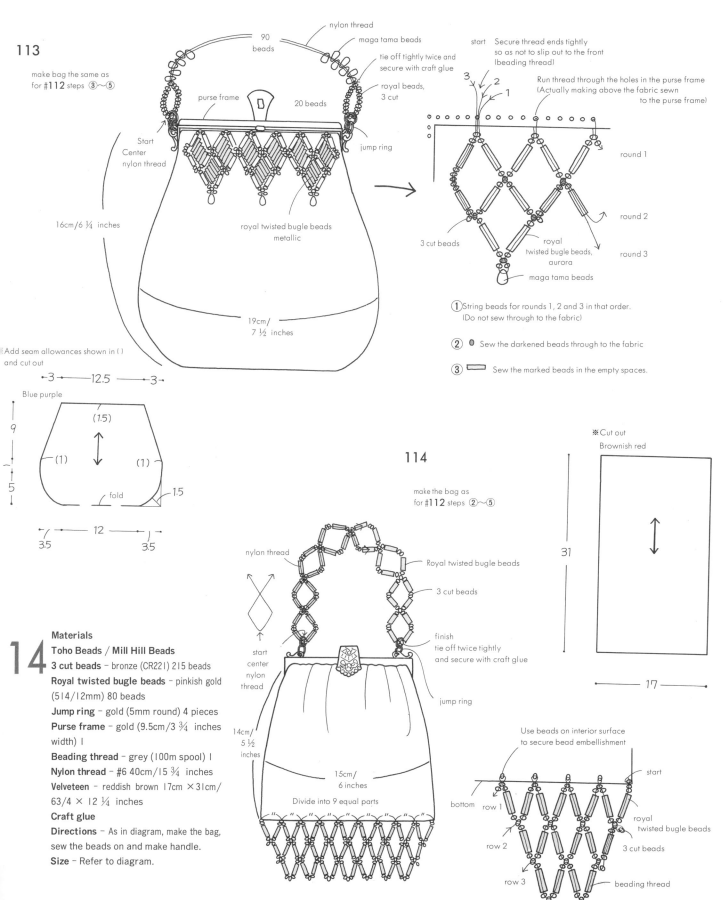

113

make bag the same as
for #112 steps ③～⑤

90 beads
nylon thread
maga tama beads
tie off tightly twice and secure with craft glue
royal beads, 3 cut

purse frame
20 beads
Start Center nylon thread
jump ring

16cm/6 ¼ inches

royal twisted bugle beads metallic

19cm/ 7 ½ inches

Add seam allowances shown in ( ) and cut out

start
Secure thread ends tightly so as not to slip out to the front (beading thread)

Run thread through the holes in the purse frame (Actually making above the fabric sewn to the purse frame)

3   2   1

round 1
round 2
round 3

3 cut beads
royal twisted bugle beads, aurora
maga tama beads

① String beads for rounds 1, 2 and 3 in that order. (Do not sew through to the fabric)

② ● Sew the darkened beads through to the fabric

③ ▭ Sew the marked beads in the empty spaces.

─ 3 ─ 12.5 ─ 3 ─

Blue purple

9

5

(1.5)
(1)   (1)
fold   1.5

─ 12 ─
3.5   3.5

114

make the bag as
for #112 steps ②～⑤

※Cut out
Brownish red

31

17

nylon thread
Royal twisted bugle beads
3 cut beads
finish tie off twice tightly and secure with craft glue
jump ring

start center nylon thread

14cm/ 5 ½ inches

15cm/ 6 inches

Divide into 9 equal parts

Use beads on interior surface to secure bead embellishment

start
bottom   row 1
row 2
row 3

royal twisted bugle beads
3 cut beads
beading thread

14

Materials

Toho Beads / Mill Hill Beads

3 cut beads – bronze (CR221) 215 beads

Royal twisted bugle beads – pinkish gold (514/12mm) 80 beads

Jump ring – gold (5mm round) 4 pieces

Purse frame – gold (9.5cm/3 ¾ inches width) 1

Beading thread – grey (100m spool) 1

Nylon thread – #6 40cm/15 ¾ inches

Velveteen – reddish brown 17cm × 31cm/ 63/4 × 12 ¼ inches

Craft glue

Directions – As in diagram, make the bag, sew the beads on and make handle.

Size – Refer to diagram.

115 mini bag

Materials

Toho Beads / Mill Hill Beads

Small round beads – light pink (11) 2377, metallic dark pink (556) 408 beads, green (246) 92 beads, metallic pink (204) 48 beads, salmon pink (923) 43 beads, pink (201) 24 beads

3 cut beads – bronze (CR222) 77 beads

TB beads – green (TB–457) 133 beads

Maga tama beads – amber (M22/4mm) 1

Acrylic beads – pink (a–286/4mm) 1

Decora beads – orange (a–5605) 1 bead

Bead cap – antique bronze 1 piece

Nylon thread – (0.2mm diameter) 180cm /70 ¾ inches

Beading thread – grey (100m spool) 1

Colored wire – (0.24mm diameter) gold 100cm/39 ½ inches

Craft glue

Directions – String beads on thread to make the body, close the bottom. String beads on thread to make the fringe and attach to the bottom. String beads on nylon thread and make the strap. String beads on wire to make motif and attach to body.

Size – Refer to diagram.

115

① Make body

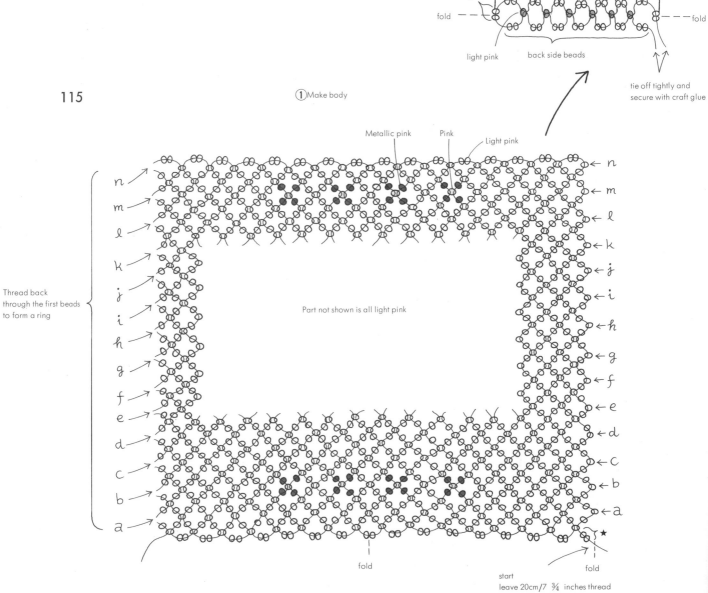

continue to close the bottom
(except for the bottom beads, beads marked light pink are used to make the body)

★

fold — — —

fold

light pink

back side beads

tie off tightly and secure with craft glue

Metallic pink   Pink   Light pink

Thread back through the first beads to form a ring

Part not shown is all light pink

n
m
l
k
j
i
h
g
f
e
d
c
b
a

← n
← m
← l
← k
← j
← i
← h
← g
← f
← e
← d
← c
← b
← a

★

fold

fold

start
leave 20cm/7 ¾ inches thread
(beading thread)

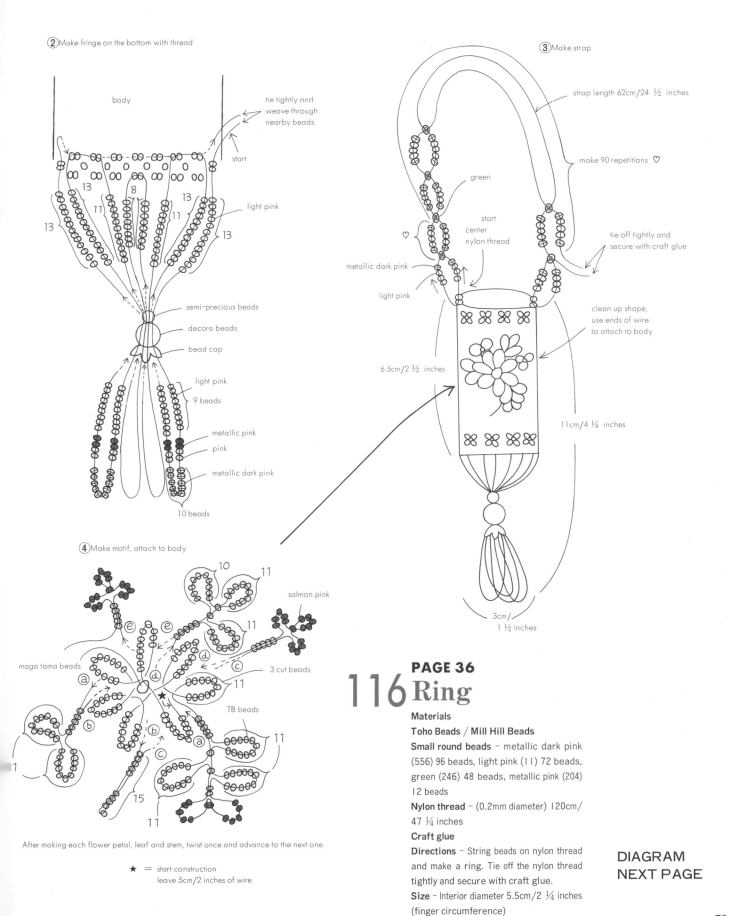

② Make fringe on the bottom with thread

body

tie tightly and
weave through
nearby beads

start

13

8

13

11

11

13

13

light pink

semi-precious beads

decora beads

bead cap

light pink

9 beads

metallic pink

pink

metallic dark pink

10 beads

③ Make strap

strap length 62cm/24 ½ inches

green

make 90 repetitions ♡

start
center
nylon thread

♡

metallic dark pink

light pink

tie off tightly and
secure with craft glue

clean up shape,
use ends of wire
to attach to body

6.5cm/2 ½ inches

11cm/4 ¼ inches

3cm/
1 ½ inches

④ Make motif, attach to body

10

11

11

salmon pink

e e

d

maga tama beads

a

d

c

3 cut beads

11

b

b

a

TB beads

c

a

11

1

15

11

After making each flower petal, leaf and stem, twist once and advance to the next one.

★ = start construction
leave 5cm/2 inches of wire

PAGE 36

116 Ring

Materials

Toho Beads / Mill Hill Beads

Small round beads – metallic dark pink
(556) 96 beads, light pink (11) 72 beads,
green (246) 48 beads, metallic pink (204)
12 beads

Nylon thread – (0.2mm diameter) 120cm/
47 ¼ inches

Craft glue

Directions – String beads on nylon thread
and make a ring. Tie off the nylon thread
tightly and secure with craft glue.

Size – Interior diameter 5.5cm/2 ¼ inches
(finger circumference)

DIAGRAM
NEXT PAGE

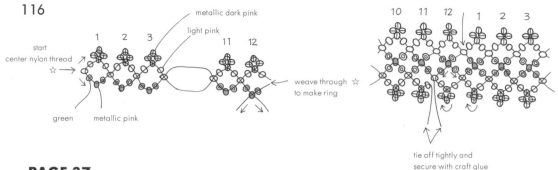

start
center nylon thread →

☆

green   metallic pink

metallic dark pink
light pink

1   2   3   11   12

weave through ☆
to make ring

10 11 12   1   2   3

tie off tightly and
secure with craft glue

PAGE 37

118 Choker

Materials

Toho Beads / Mill Hill Beads

Small round beads – gun metal (81) 419 beads, grey (9) 110 beads, pink (267) 90 beads

3 cut beads – bronze (CR222) 317 beads

Large round beads – grey (9) 2 beads

Round pearl – dark gun metal 6mm – 1bead, 8mm – 2 beads, bronze 3mm – 2 beads

Faceted glass beads – grey (a–5309/ 4mm) 2 beads

Crystal cut beads – amethyst (J–54/ 4mm/#8) 2 beads

Metal beads – antique silver (a–7201SF) 2 beads

Retro beads – antique silver (a–359SF) 2 beads

Acrylic cut beads – purple (a–264/ 6mm) 2 beads

Colored wire – (0.24mm diameter) silver 400cm/157 ½ inches

Bead cap (large) – antique silver 9 beads

Bead cap (small) – antique silver 5 beads

Head pin – bronze (22mm) 7 pins

Eye pin – bronze (30mm) 2 pins

Jump ring (3.8mm round) – bronze 13

pieces

Jump ring (5mm round) – bronze 2 pieces

Lobster clasp – bronze 1

Cable chain – bronze 40cm/15 ¾ inches

Pierced surface pin back – silver (14mm) 1

Felt – black 2cm × 2cm/¾ × ¾ inch

Black thread – some

Directions – Pull tightly on the wire while making individual parts, keeping left right symmetry in mind. Attach parts to the pierced surface according to diagram. Attach remaining parts.

Size – 41cm/16 ¼ inches

118

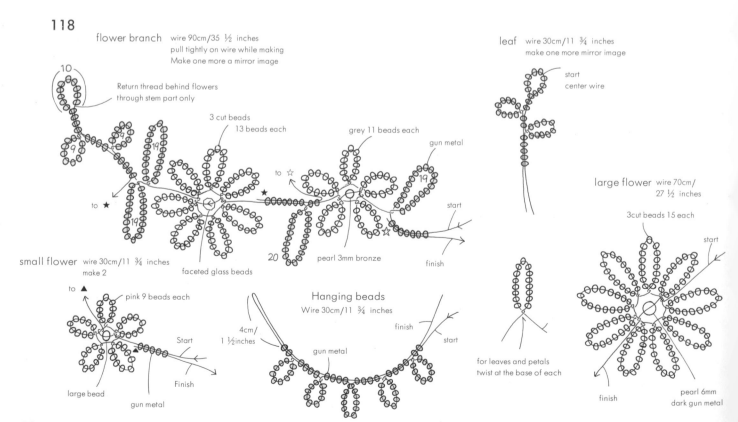

flower branch   wire 90cm/35 ½ inches
pull tightly on wire while making
Make one more a mirror image

10

Return thread behind flowers
through stem part only

19

19

to ★

3 cut beads
13 beads each

to ☆

★

grey 11 beads each
gun metal

19

start

19

20

faceted glass beads

pearl 3mm bronze

finish

leaf   wire 30cm/11 ¾ inches
make one more mirror image

start
center wire

large flower   wire 70cm/ 27 ½ inches

3cut beads 15 each

start

small flower   wire 30cm/11 ¾ inches
make 2

to ▲

pink 9 beads each

Start

Finish

large bead

gun metal

Hanging beads
Wire 30cm/11 ¾ inches

4cm/ 1 ½inches

gun metal

finish

start

for leaves and petals
twist at the base of each

finish

pearl 6mm
dark gun metal

jump ring 5mm

jump ring 3.8mm

chain 5cm/2 inches

lobster clasp

Back view

Thread wire through the pierced surface, twist several together and trim excess.

leaves

Flower branch

Flower branch

Small flower

Small flower

Hanging beads

※ Use only
the pierced surface of the pin

Sew a piece of felt the size
of the pierced surface to the back.

chain 12cm/4 ¾ inches

chain 12cm/4 ¾ inches

flower branch

leaf

leaf (large)

Bead cap (large)

Retro beads

Bead cap (large)

Head pin

Bead cap (small)

Metal bead

Bead cap (large)

Crystal cut bead

Gun metal

small flower

bead cap (large)

pearl 8mm dark gun metal

bead cap (small)

bead cap (large)

head pin

hanging beads

Eye pin

Head pin

acrylic cut bead

bead cap (small)

Thread wire through the pierced surface
to attach in the following order:
flower branch, leaf, small flower, hanging beads,
large flower. Attach decorations and chain.

PAGE 37
119 Comb

Materials

Toho Beads / Mill Hill Beads

Small round beads – gun metal (81) 206 beads, grey (9) & pink (267) 56 beads each

3 cut beads – bronze (CR222) 196 beads

Large round beads – grey (9) 2 beads

Round pearl – dark gun metal 3mm – 2 beads, 4mm – 1 bead, 6mm – 2 beads, bronze 3mm – 2 beads

Colored wire – (0.24mm diameter) silver 180cm/70 ¾ inches

15 toothed comb – silver (55mm) 1

Directions – Pull wire tightly while making flowers symmetrically right and left. Finish by attaching to comb.

Size – Refer to diagram.

use the wire remaining on both ends
to wrap around attaching to comb.
Attach 6mm pearls during this process

pearl 6mm
dark gunmetal

pearl 6mm
dark gun metal

119

※ pull wire tightly while making

3 cut beads
9 bead each

gun metal

grey

pink

center flower

3 cut beads
11 beads each

From the center flower
make a mirror image
to the right

13

finish
use to
attach to comb

pearl 3mm
dark gun metal

pearl 3mm
bronze

small round
beads

Thread through ☆・★
for each and continue

pearl 4mm
dark gun metal

start

center wire

for leaves and petals
twist at the base after making each

twist

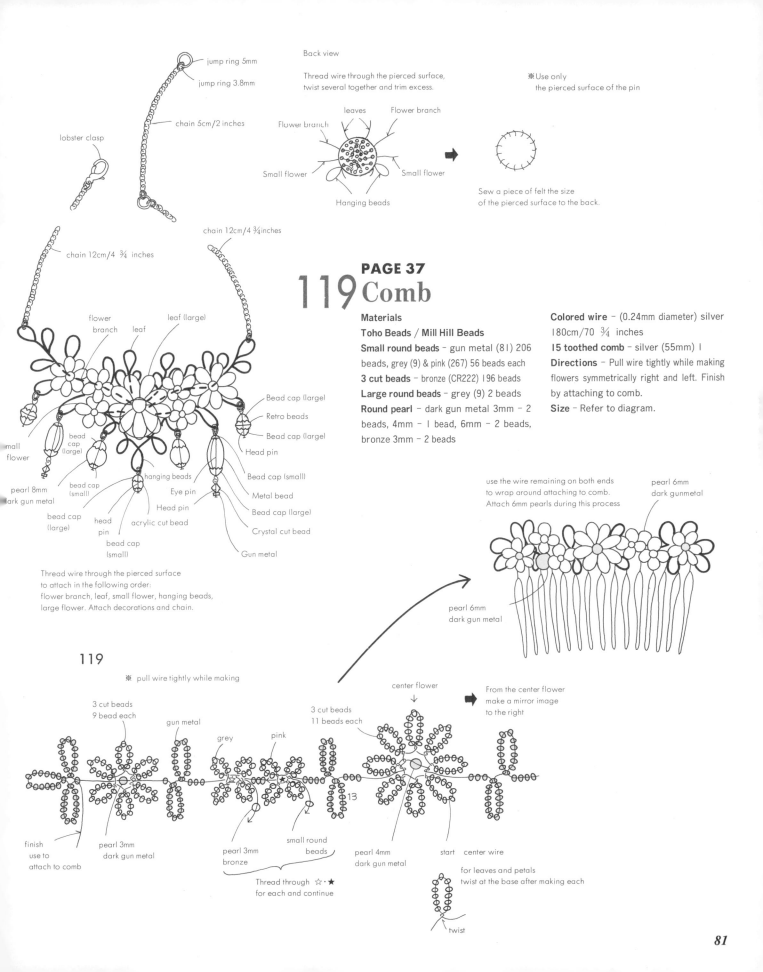

120 Ring

Materials

Toho Beads / Mill Hill Beads

Small round beads – gun metal (81) 75 beads, grey (9) 36 beads, pink (267) 28 beads

3 cut beads – bronze (CR222) 73 beads

Large round beads – grey (9) 1 bead

Round pearl – dark gun metal (3mm) 1 bead, bronze (3mm) 2 beads

Faceted glass beads – purple (a-5308/4mm) 1 bead

Retro beads – antique silver (a-359SF) 1 bead

Colored wire (0.24mm diameter) – silver 125cm/49 ¼ inches

Nylon thread – (0.3mm diameter) 40cm/15 ¾ inches

Bead cap (large) – antique silver 2 beads

Pierced surface pin back – silver (14mm) 1

Felt – black 2cm × 2cm/3/4 × ¾ inch

Black thread – some

Craft glue

Directions – Pull wire tightly while constructing the various parts. Use the pierced surface from the pin, attach the ring as shown in the diagram and then the various parts.

Size – Interior diameter 5.5cm/2 ½ inches (finger circumference)

120

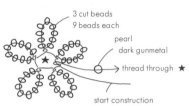

antique gold flower

3 cut beads
9 beads each

pearl
dark gunmetal

→ thread through ★

start construction

pink flower
grey flower } bead 1

make 1 each as for earring #**121**

bead 2

pearl bronze

faceted glass beads

wire 10cm/4 inches

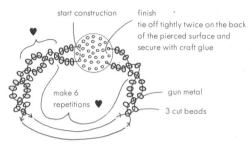

ring   nylon thread 40cm/15 ¾ inches

start construction

finish
tie off tightly twice on the back of the pierced surface and secure with craft glue

make 6 repetitions ♥

gun metal

3 cut beads

121 Earring

Materials

Toho Beads / Mill Hill Beads

Small round beads – grey (9) 72 beads, pink (267) 56 beads, gun metal (81) 54 beads

3 cut beads – bronze (CR222) 80 beads

Large round beads – grey (9) 2 beads

Round pearl – dark gun metal (3mm), bronze (3mm) & silver (3mm) 2 beads each

Faceted glass beads – purple (a-5308/4mm) 2 beads

Retro beads – antique silver (a-359SF) 2 beads

Colored wire (0.24mm diameter) – silver 240cm/94 ½ inches

Bead cap (large) – antique silver 4 pieces

Pierced surface earring finding – silver 1 set

Directions – Pull wire tightly while constructing the various parts. Attach to the pierced surface as per diagram. Attach pierced surface to earring finding. Make one more a mirror image.

Size – Refer to diagram.

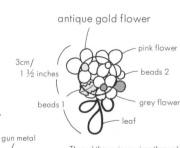

pink flower

leaf

beads 2

grey flower

antique gold flower

beads 1

Made with the same techniques as choker **118**. Arrange flowers and leaves on pierced surface for balance and secure in the back.

※use only the pierced surface from the pierced surface pin set

121

flower and leaves wire 25cm/9 ¾ inches make 2 each
beads 1 & 2 wire 10cm/4 inches, make 2 each

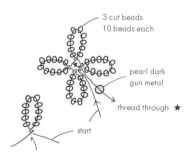

Antique gold flower

3 cut beads
10 beads each

pearl dark gun metal

thread through ★

start

flowers and leaves, twist at the base after making each one

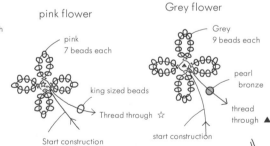

pink flower

pink
7 beads each

king sized beads

Thread through ☆

Start construction

Grey flower

Grey
9 beads each

pearl bronze

thread through ▲

start construction

beads 1

bead cap (large)

retro bead

Beads 2

Pearl silver

Faceted glass beads

leaf

gun metal

7 beads

7 beads

9 beads

start construction

antique gold flower

3cm/
1 ½ inches

pink flower

beads 2

beads 1

grey flower

leaf

Thread the various wires through the hole in the pierced surface and secure.
Fold down the lugs of the pierced surface to attach to the earring finding.

Make one more a mirror image.

22 PAGE 38 Bracelet

Materials

Toho Beads / Mill Hill Beads

Small round beads – black (49) 396 beads, gun metal (81) 178 beads

Black pearl – (3mm) 32 beads, (4mm) 3 beads

Crystal cut beads – black (J–54/4mm/#10) 8 beads

Colored wire – (0.35~0.37mm diameter) silver 160cm/63 inches

Nylon thread – (0.2mm diameter) 150cm/59 inches

Clasp set – bronze 1 set

Craft glue

Directions – Thread beads on wire and make butterfly. String beads on nylon thread to make the finger loop and the bracelet. Attach clasp.

Size – Refer to diagram.

23 PAGE 38 Necklace

Materials

Toho Beads / Mill Hill Beads

Small round beads – gun metal (81) 564 beads, black (49) 377 beads

Black pearl – (3mm) 30 beads, (4mm) 3 beads

Crystal cut beads – black (J–54/4mm/#10) 13 beads

Colored wire – (0.35~0.37mm diameter) silver 160cm/63 inches

Nylon thread – (0.2mm diameter) 270cm/106 ¼ inches

Clasp set – bronze 1 set

Jump ring – bronze (3.8mm round) 2 pieces

Head pin – antique silver (22mm) 2 pieces

Craft glue

Directions – Thread beads on wire and make butterfly. Thread beads on head pin and attach to butterfly. Thread beads on nylon thread to make choker. Attach clasp.

Size – Refer to diagram.

DIAGRAM ON NEXT PAGE

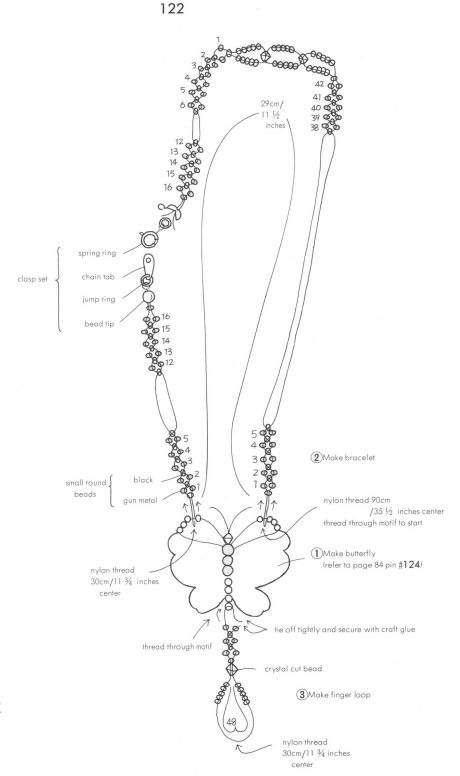

122

clasp set
- spring ring
- chain tab
- jump ring
- bead tip

29cm/11 ½ inches

small round beads
- black
- gun metal

nylon thread 30cm/11 ¾ inches center

thread through motif

② Make bracelet

nylon thread 90cm /35 ½ inches center thread through motif to start

① Make butterfly (refer to page 84 pin #124)

tie off tightly and secure with craft glue

crystal cut bead

③ Make finger loop

nylon thread 30cm/11 ¾ inches center

124 Pin

Materials

Toho Beads / Mill Hill Beads

Small round beads – gun metal (81) 134
bead, black (49) 42 beads

Royal beads – silver (711) 96 beads

Black pearl – 3mm – 30 beads, 4mm – 3
beads

Crystal cut beads – black (J–54/4mm/
#10) 7 beads

Colored wire – (0.35～0.37mm diameter)
silver 180cm/70 ¾ inches

Pin back with rotating clasp – bronze 1

Directions – Thread beads on wire to
make butterfly. Use separate wire to
attach pin backing to the back.

Size – Refer to diagram.

Antenna

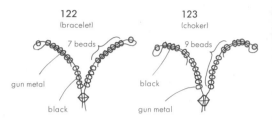

122
(bracelet)
7 beads
gun metal
black

123
(choker)
9 beads
black
gun metal

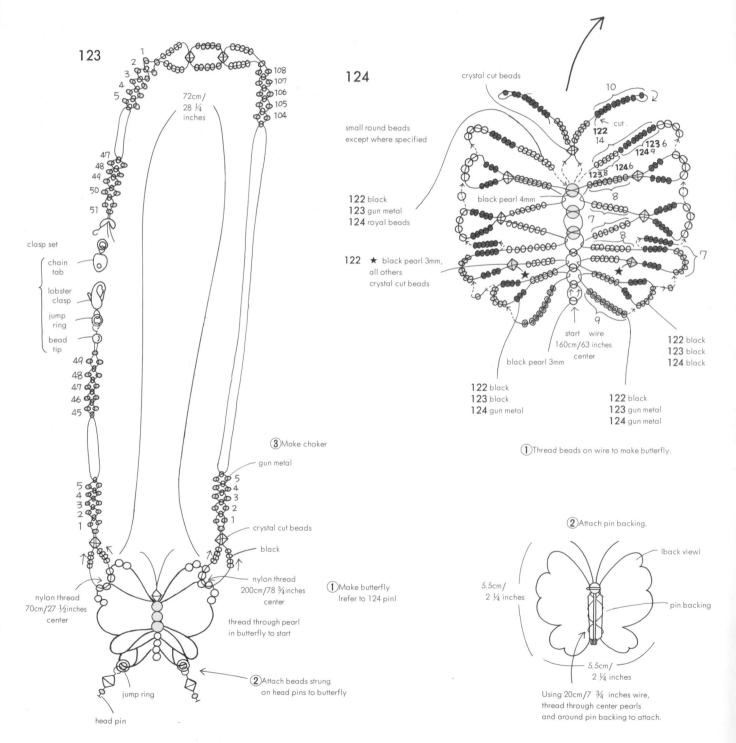

123

1
2
3
4
5

72cm/
28 ¼
inches

108
107
106
105
104

47
48
49
50
51

clasp set

chain tab

lobster clasp

jump ring

bead tip

49
48
47
46
45

③ Make choker

gun metal

5
4
3
2
1

crystal cut beads

black

nylon thread
200cm/78 ¾ inches
center

thread through pearl
in butterfly to start

5
4
3
2
1

nylon thread
70cm/27 ½ inches
center

jump ring

head pin

① Make butterfly
(refer to 124 pin)

② Attach beads strung
on head pins to butterfly

124

small round beads
except where specified

122 black
123 gun metal
124 royal beads

122 ★ black pearl 3mm,
all others
crystal cut beads

crystal cut beads

10

cut.

122
14

123 6
124 9

123 8   124 6

black pearl 4mm

8

7

8

7

start wire
160cm/63 inches
center

9

black pearl 3mm

122 black
123 black
124 gun metal

122 black
123 black
124 gun metal

122 black
123 black
124 black

122 black
123 gun metal
124 gun metal

① Thread beads on wire to make butterfly.

② Attach pin backing.

(back view)

5.5cm/
2 ¼ inches

pin backing

5.5cm/
2 ¼ inches

Using 20cm/7 ¾ inches wire,
thread through center pearls
and around pin backing to attach.

25 Bag

Materials

Toho Beads / Mill Hill Beads

Royal beads – silver (711) 62 beads

Black pearl – 3mm – 129 beads, 4mm – 31 beads

Jump ring – bronze (5mm round) 2 pieces

Eye pin – antique silver (30mm) 31 pins

Purse frame – silver (12.5cm/5 inches width) 1

Black velour – 57cm × 19.5cm/22 ½ inches × 7 ¾ inches

Lining fabric – 57cm × 19.5cm/22 ½ inches × 7 ¾ inches

Interfacing – 57cm × 19.5cm/22 ½ inches × 7 ¾ inches

Directions – Cut out fabric. Affix interfacing to fabric. Make tucks in the body of the bag and sew on the heading. Make outside and lining. Sew to the purse frame. Make the strap and attach to the purse frame.

Size – Refer to diagram.

125

① Add 1cm/ ½ inch seam allowance and cut out fabric

heading, body, lining and interfacing 2 each

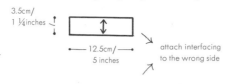

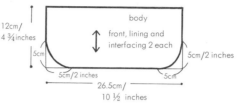

② Make tucks in body

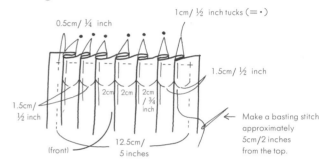

⑤ When lining is finished, turn under the edges and sew to the inside of the purse frame.

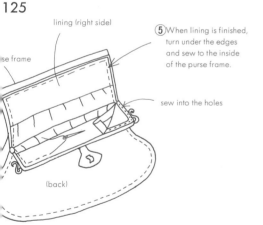

sew into the holes

③ Sew the heading and the body with right sides together. Remove the basting threads from tucks.

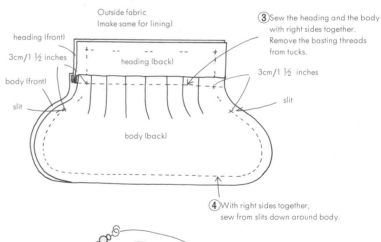

④ With right sides together, sew from slits down around body.

⑥ Turn right side out, fold. Sew pearls to right side while attaching to purse frame.

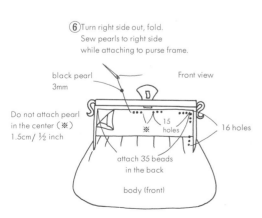

⑦ Make strap and attach to the purse frame

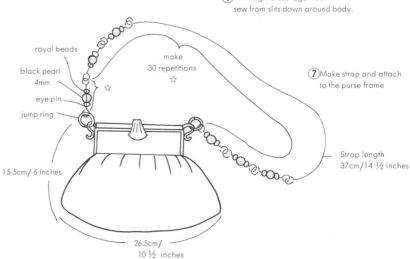

86 PAGE 25 Bracelet

Materials

Toho Beads / Mill Hill Beads

3 cut beads − red (CR400) 122 beads

Metal parts, joint − antique silver 8 beads

Jump ring (5mm round) − bronze 4 pieces

Jump ring (3.8mm round) − bronze 35 pieces

Eye pin − antique silver (30mm) 14 pins

Clasp set − bronze 1 set

Directions − Thread beads on eye pins and assemble parts with jump rings.

Size − 18cm/7 inches

89

Materials

Toho Beads / Mill Hill Beads

3 cut beads − blue (CR163) 54 beads

Metal parts, joint − bronze 10 pieces

Jump ring − bronze (3.8mm round) 20 pieces

Eye pin − antique silver (30mm) 9 pins

Clasp set − bronze 1 set

Directions − Make as for bracelet #87.

Size − 18cm/7 inches

93 PAGE 26 Comb

Materials

Toho Beads / Mill Hill Beads

Small round beads − green (324) 80 beads, blue (952) 40 beads

Bugle beads − bronze (222/6mm) 21 beads

Nylon thread − (0.3mm diameter) 150cm/ 59 inches

15 toothed comb − gold (55mm) 1

Craft glue

Directions − Make as for bracelet #87.

Size − 4.5cm/1 ¾ inches high

94

Materials

Toho Beads / Mill Hill Beads

Small round beads − blue (243) 80 beads, salmon pink (955) 40 beads

Bugle beads − bronze (222/6mm) 21 beads

Nylon thread − (0.3mm diameter) 150cm/ 59 inches

15 toothed comb − silver (55mm) 1

Craft glue

Directions − Make as for comb #93.

Size − 4.5cm/1 ¾ inches high.

87

Materials

Toho Beads / Mill Hill Beads

3 cut beads − metallic (CR244) 54 beads

Metal parts, joint − silver 10 pieces

Jump ring − silver (3.8mm round) 20 pieces

Eye pin − antique silver (30mm) 9 pins

Clasp set − bronze 1 set

Directions − Thread beads on eye pins and assemble parts with jump rings.

Size − 18cm/7 inches

88

Materials

Toho Beads / Mill Hill Beads

3 cut beads − crystal (CR161) 54 beads

Metal parts, joint − gold 10 pieces

Jump rings − gold (3.8mm round) 20 pieces

Eye pin − antique gold (30mm) 9 pins

Clasp set − bronze 1 set

Directions − Make as for bracelet #87.

Size − 18cm/7 inches

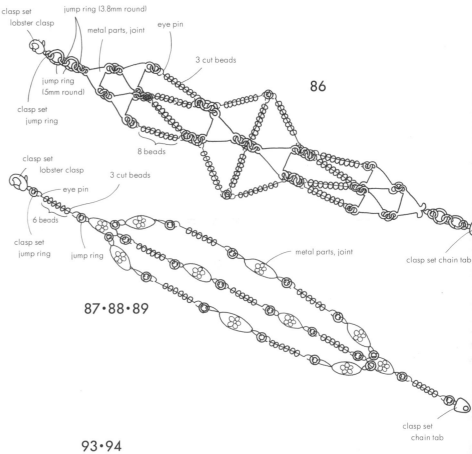

clasp set lobster clasp

jump ring (3.8mm round)

metal parts, joint

eye pin

3 cut beads

jump ring (5mm round)

clasp set jump ring

86

8 beads

clasp set chain tab

clasp set lobster clasp

3 cut beads

eye pin

6 beads

clasp set jump ring

jump ring

metal parts, joint

87·88·89

clasp set chain tab

93·94

93 green 94 blue

93 blue 94 salmon pink

bugle beads

end of woven pattern
tie twice tightly and secure with craft glue

start
center nylon thread

comb

Use the leftover pieces of nylon thread to wrap around the comb and motif to attach. At the end of the motif, tie off tightly twice and secure with craft glue.

●Tools and Findings

Snipe nosed pliers

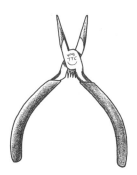

In addition to cutting wire, they can be used to open and close rings, metal parts and to curve the end of pins. If there are 2 available, it is convenient to use one in each hand. One variety has thin points for easily picking up items and another type which has one side rounded for easy curving of pins.

Round nosed pliers

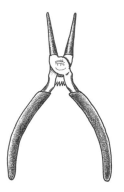

The tips are thin and round. Useful for curving the tips of pins.

Pliers

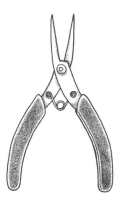

The ends are like tweezers, making it a convenient tool.

Beading Needles and Needle Threads

Bead craft needles are characterized by being long, thin and having small eyes.

Wire & Nylon Thread

Leaving 5~10cm/2~4 inches extra, and using cellophane tape to make a temporary anchor before starting helps to secure the nylon thread and makes it easier to work with.

Beading Thread

Thread used for accessories resists breakage and is strong.

Craft Glue

Use for tidying up the tied ends of threads.

Scissors

Pliers which have a cutting edge (Nipper) are best, but a sturdy pair of scissors which can cut pins and chains is sufficient.

Cellophane Tape

Useful for making a temporary anchor for nylon thread to begin construction.

Jump Rings

Jump rings come in circles, small ovals and a variety of sizes. They are used to connect metal parts. When opening slide to the side rather than opening out. When closing take care that no space remains open and the ends do not overlap.

when opening   when closing

Clasps

-500

spring ring   jump ring (round)

chain tab   bead tip

-501

lobster clasp

chain tab

Bead Tips

When Attaching a Single String

Bead tip

Wrap the string as in the diagram, tie a knot larger than the hole in the bead tip. Apply craft glue to the surface of the knot and close the bead tip.

When Attaching 2 Strings

Small round bead

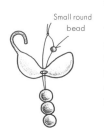

Thread a small bead or crimp tube as in the diagram, tie the beads in an overhand knot twice, apply craft glue to the surface of the knot and close the bead tip.

Crimp Tubes

Place inside bead tip

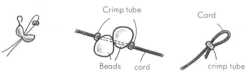

Used to secure a string bead or tidy up the end of a cord. Fix by squeezing together with pliers.

Using Eye Pins and Head Pins

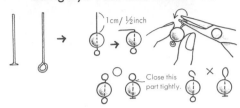

After stringing beads, trim leaving 1cm/ ½ inch Using pliers, bend to the side before rounding it out. As much as possible close tightly leaving no space.

Skillful Twisting of Wir

Do not try to twist the whole wire once. Hold at the base of the be and twist down 2~3mm at a time.

Pierced Surface Findings

These findings resemble shower heads. Using thread or nylon thread to attach beads to surface, attach the ring or earring base and fold the lugs to secure.

How to String Beads

When using fine nylon thread or thread a needle is used. Thick nylon thread can be used as is. Cellophane tape is used as a temporary anchor at the beginning. When stringing a number of pre-strung beads, transfer directly.

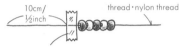

Use cellophane tape to secure

● Pick up on the needle

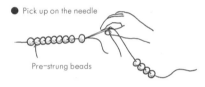

Pre-strung beads

● Tying strings together to transfer

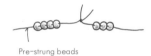

Pre-strung beads

Adding More Thread

Tie threads tightly together. Additionally app adhesive (for thread use craft glue, for nylon thre use instant adhesive) to the surface. When t adhesive has dried, thread bead over the kno

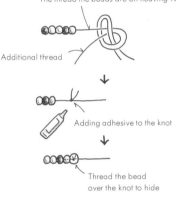

When Making Accessories

As wire dents easily, be careful not to bend the wire. (Wire breaks easily at dents and bends) Also, as the wire tends to unravel from the roll, sticking a piece of cellophane tape as shown in the diagram is helpful.

When using beads, lay a piece of felt in a small dish or container to keep them from rolling around. Make selections from container.

Taking care of beaded accessories

Summer is a time in which the opportunity wear accessories next to the skin increases, if left soiled and dusty, they can change co and deteriorate. Clean after each use with dry, soft cloth lightly wipe to remove. This alo will improve the life of accessories. Use jewe cleaning cloths to wipe clasps, earring findir and so on.

When You Find You Have Made a Mistake in Bead Stringing

Grasp with pliers and crush. Or crush with an awl. (Avoid doing this with expensive beads.)

Crush on top of a plastic bag

Crush with an awl.

Eraser

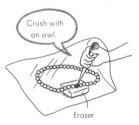

Fitting a ring for size

Check against finger for size while making.

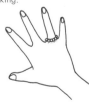

Wrap around finger to view. Determine the number of beads according to finger size.

Making Necklace to Size

Before affixing clasp, try around the neck to determine the number of beads.